101
BEST
DIET
FOODS

Betsy A. Hornick, MS, RD

Publications International, Ltd.

Betsy A. Hornick, M.S., R.D., is a registered dietitian specializing in nutrition education and communications. She has written and edited numerous nutrition and health education publications for both consumers and health professionals, including materials published by the American Dietetic Association. She is co-author of The Healthy Beef Cookbook and a regular contributor to Diabetic Cooking magazine.

Recipes pictured on the front cover: Tuscan Style Sausage Skillet *(page 81)* and New Wave Chicken Salad Wraps *(page 105).*

Recipe pictured on the back cover: Grilled Pork Tenderloin with Apple Salsa *(page 11).*

Photo Credits

Cover Art: Media Bakery; PIL Collection and Shutterstock.

Interior Art: Dreamstime, iStock Photo, Media Bakery, PIL Collection, Shutterstock and Thinkstock

ISBN-13: 978-1-4508-2269-5
ISBN-10: 1-4508-2269-X

Library of Congress Control Number: 2011931800

Manufactured in China.

8 7 6 5 4 3 2 1

Nutritional Analysis: Every effort has been made to check the accuracy of the nutritional information that appears with each recipe. However, because numerous variables account for a wide range of values for certain foods, nutritive analyses in this book should be considered approximate. Different results may be obtained by using different nutrient databases and different brand-name products.

Microwave Cooking: Microwave ovens vary in wattage. Use the cooking times as guidelines and check for doneness before adding more time.

Note: This book is for informational purposes and is not intended to provide medical advice. Neither Publications International, Ltd., nor the author, editors, or publisher take responsibility for any possible consequences from any treatment, procedure, exercise, dietary modification, action, or application of medication or preparation by any person reading or following the information in this book. The publication of this book does not constitute the practice of medicine, and this book does not attempt to replace your physician, pharmacist, or other health care provider. **Before undertaking any course of treatment, the author, editors, and publisher advise the reader to check with a physician or other health care provider.**

Publications International, Ltd.

Food Can Help You Lose Weight!

Today's approach to losing weight is less about what you shouldn't eat and more about what you should eat. It's a positive focus that encourages you to explore the vast array of foods that are nutritious and delicious and that also support your weight-loss efforts and goals.

The foods featured in *101 Best Diet Foods* all have some key qualities that can help you slim down.

Some of the foods provide nutrients that help you manage your hunger by filling you up more quickly and helping to prevent you from overeating. There are also foods that are tasty on their own and those that are flavor enhancers so you won't even miss any of the fat-laden foods that can compromise your diet. Plus, many of the foods provide additional health benefits.

You may have heard that it's important to eat more whole foods. That's true, especially when you're watching your weight. This means building your diet around minimally processed foods, such as fruits and vegetables, whole grains, low-fat and fat-free milk products and lean meats. There's also growing evidence that eating sufficient

amounts of fiber, complex carbohydrates, protein, essential vitamins and minerals and phytonutrients (naturally occurring plant nutrients) from whole foods can help lower the risk of common diseases, including heart disease, high blood pressure, cancer and diabetes.

101 Best Diet Foods doesn't just provide you with foods that are good for you and your waistline. It also tells you how to choose and store them, gives tips for healthy preparation and serving and offers recipes so you can prepare delicious and healthy dishes. To get the most from the foods in this book, keep in mind these important points:

1. Aim high when it comes to variety.
Although 101 is a good number, it's certainly not the limit of good-for-you foods. Use these foods as a stepping stone to exploring even more options. Nutrient information per serving is provided for each food to help you make comparisons.

2. Select and store foods wisely. Learn how to shop for the freshest and healthiest varieties of foods featured in this book. When you select the best, you are more likely to get the most nutrients from your foods and most importantly, enjoy eating them. Likewise, proper storage of foods is important to ensure the best quality and safety of what you eat.

3. Use smart preparation strategies. To keep foods healthy and lower in calories, take some time to learn strategies for preparing specific foods, especially those you have not tried before. You may even learn some new tips about preparing foods that you eat often. By trying new and different ways to prepare foods, you will look forward to eating them again.

4. Be adventurous with recipes. The best way to experiment with unfamiliar foods is to use a recipe that brings out the foods' greatest qualities. The same is true for foods you eat every day. Be adventurous and try some of the recipes in this book to learn new ways to serve and enjoy your food. Nutrients per serving are provided for each recipe to help you fit these foods in your overall diet.

Acorn Squash

This acorn-shaped variety of winter squash is full of flavor and nutrients. It is easy to find during fall and winter months and simple to prepare. It is most commonly baked and has slightly sweet flesh that is high in fiber.

benefits

The high fiber content makes acorn squash particularly satisfying and a good addition to a weight-loss plan. Acorn squash is rich in vitamin A (beta-carotene), vitamin C and potassium, which helps control blood pressure.

selection and storage

Acorn squash is available year-round, although it is best from early fall to late winter. Look for acorn squash that are deeply colored (dark green with some golden coloring) and free of spots, bruises and mold. The hard skin of winter squash serves as a barrier, allowing it to be stored a month or more in a cool, dark place.

preparation and serving tips

Acorn squash can be baked, steamed, sautéed, simmered or microwaved. One of the easiest ways to prepare it is to cut one in half, scoop out the seeds and bake for about 45 minutes. Season it and serve plain in the skin or fill the center with rice, barley, legumes or pine nuts. Or scoop out the baked flesh, mash it and sprinkle with a small amount of Parmesan cheese or other seasonings. Enjoy as a side dish or make a filled half of acorn squash the center of your meal. Acorn squash is also delicious in savory soups.

nutrients per serving:

Acorn Squash
½ cup cooked

Calories 57 **Protein** 1g **Total Fat** 0g
Saturated Fat 0g **Cholesterol** 0mg
Carbohydrate 15g **Dietary Fiber** 4.5g
Sodium 0mg **Potassium** 450mg
Calcium 45mg **Iron** 0.9mg
Vitamin A 439 IU **Vitamin C** 11mg
Folate 19mcg

glazed maple acorn squash

1 large acorn or golden acorn squash
¼ cup water
2 tablespoons pure maple syrup
1 tablespoon margarine or butter, melted
¼ teaspoon ground cinnamon

1. Preheat oven to 375°F. Cut ends from squash; cut squash crosswise into four or five equal slices. Discard seeds and membrane.

2. Place water in 13×9-inch baking dish. Arrange squash in dish; cover with foil. Bake 30 minutes or until tender.

3. Combine maple syrup, margarine and cinnamon in small bowl; mix well. Uncover squash; drain. Brush squash with syrup mixture, letting excess pool in center of squash rings.

4. Bake 10 minutes or until bubbly.

Makes 4 servings

nutrients per serving:

Calories 90
Calories from Fat 30%
Protein 1g
Carbohydrate 18g
Fiber 2g
Total Fat 3g
Saturated Fat 1g
Cholesterol 8mg
Sodium 39mg

Almonds

Almonds are the seeds of the fruit from an almond tree. The almond seed is loaded with nutrients, most notably vitamin E, protein and healthy monounsaturated fat. We do not eat the outer fruit.

benefits

The combination of protein, fiber and heart-healthy fats found in almonds makes them a great filling snack for dieters, staving off hunger. Almonds fit into many popular weight-loss plans, but watch your portions because calories can add up quickly. Almonds are an excellent source of vitamin E and magnesium, and provide calcium, too.

selection and storage

You can buy almonds in the shell, but shelled almonds are available packaged or in bulk. Packaged almonds are available in various forms—blanched (to remove the skin), raw, whole, sliced, slivered, dry or oil roasted, salted or unsalted, smoked and flavored. Always check for a freshness date on packaged almonds. Unshelled almonds can keep for a few months in a cool, dry place. Once they're shelled or a package is opened, you will need to refrigerate or freeze them.

preparation and serving tips

Almonds are versatile and can be sprinkled on salads, soups, casseroles, vegetables, stir-fries, cereal and more. As a snack, stick with 1 ounce, (about a handful or 23 almonds). Try roasting them in the oven to intensify their flavor.

nutrients per serving:

Almonds, dry roasted without salt
1 ounce

Calories 169 **Protein** 6g
Total Fat 15g **Saturated Fat** 1g
Cholesterol 0mg **Carbohydrate** 6g
Dietary Fiber 3g **Sodium** 0mg
Potassium 200mg **Calcium** 76mg
Iron 1mg **Vitamin A** 0 IU
Vitamin C 0mg **Folate** 15mcg
Vitamin E 7mg **Magnesium** 80mg

almond-oat thins

¼ **cup blanched slivered almonds**
2 **tablespoons sugar**
¼ **cup plus 1 tablespoon quick oats, divided**
¼ **cup flour**
3 **tablespoons soft butter spread with oil**
2 **egg whites**
¼ **cup light corn syrup**
½ **teaspoon vanilla**
¼ **teaspoon almond extract**

1. Preheat oven to 350°F. Line baking sheets with parchment paper or nonstick silicone baking mats.

2. Place almonds and sugar in food processor; process using 3-second pulses until mixture resembles coarse meal. Add ¼ cup oats; process using 3-second pulses until finely ground. Add flour; pulse two to three times. *Do not overmix.*

3. Beat butter in large bowl with electric mixer at medium speed until creamy. Add egg whites, corn syrup, vanilla and almond extract; beat 1 minute.

4. Add dry mixture and remaining 1 tablespoon oats to butter mixture; beat at low speed until well blended.

5. Drop batter by level teaspoonfuls 2 inches apart onto prepared baking sheets. Using back of wet spoon, spread batter into thin 2½-inch rounds.

6. Bake 8 minutes or until golden. Remove cookies to wire rack to cool completely.

Makes 36 servings (1 cookie per serving)

nutrients per serving:

Calories 30
Calories from Fat 60%
Protein 1g
Carbohydrate 4g
Fiber <1g
Total Fat 2g
Saturated Fat <1g
Cholesterol 0mg
Sodium 19mg

Apples

There are thousands of apple varieties grown today. Flavors range from sweet to tart, colors from yellow and green to deep red and textures from tender to crisp. And they are a great low-fat, fiber-packed food that can be enjoyed in many different ways.

benefits

Apples are the perfect addition to your weight-loss plan because they are low in calories and high in fiber. Whether eaten as a snack or in a sweet, crunchy salad, they can be a key food in your diet. The soluble fiber in apples also helps lower cholesterol levels. Eating an apple before a meal is a good way to curb your appetite and prevent you from overindulging.

selection and storage

Choose apples for their intended purpose. A few varieties, like Golden Delicious, Jonathan and Winesap, are all-purpose apples. For baking, try Empire, Rome Beauty, Cortland, Northern Spy or Ida Red; they deliver flavor and keep their shape when cooked. For just plain eating, you can't beat Gala, Fuji, Braeburn or Honeycrisp. Apples prefer humid air, so the crisper drawer of the refrigerator is the best place to store them. Some varieties will keep for several months, though most get mealy within a month or two.

preparation and serving tips

Always wash your apples. Supermarket apples are often waxed, which seals in pesticide residues that may be on the skins. Peeling apples will remove the film but also a lot of the fiber. To prevent browning, sprinkle a little lemon juice on cut surfaces.

nutrients per serving:

Apple
1 medium

Calories 95
Protein <1g
Total Fat 0g
Saturated Fat 0g
Cholesterol 0g
Carbohydrate 25g
Dietary Fiber 4g
Sodium 0mg
Potassium 195mg
Calcium 11mg
Iron 0.2mg
Vitamin A 98 IU
Vitamin C 8mg
Folate 5mcg

nutrients per serving:

Calories 201
Calories from Fat 21%
Protein 26g

Carbohydrate 14g
Fiber 2g
Total Fat 5g

Saturated Fat 1g
Cholesterol 81mg
Sodium 678mg

grilled pork tenderloin with apple salsa

- 1 tablespoon chili powder
- ½ teaspoon garlic powder
- 1 pound pork tenderloin
- 2 Granny Smith apples, peeled, cored and finely chopped
- 1 can (4 ounces) diced mild green chiles
- ¼ cup lemon juice
- 3 tablespoons finely chopped fresh cilantro
- 1 clove garlic, minced
- 1 teaspoon dried oregano
- ½ teaspoon salt

1. Spray grid with nonstick cooking spray. Preheat grill to medium-high heat.

2. Combine chili powder and garlic powder in small bowl; mix well. Coat pork with spice mixture.

3. Grill pork 30 minutes, turning occasionally, until barely pink in center (165°F). Transfer to cutting board; tent with foil and let stand 10 to 15 minutes before slicing. Internal temperature will continue to rise 5°F to 10°F during stand time.

4. Meanwhile, combine apples, chiles, lemon juice, cilantro, garlic, oregano and salt in medium bowl; mix well.

5. Slice pork across grain; serve with salsa. *Makes 4 servings*

Artichokes

Fibrous artichokes are a dieter's delight—they have a buttery, delicate flavor yet are fat free and high in fiber. Artichokes can be enjoyed alone or incorporated into salads or pasta dishes.

nutrients per serving:

**Artichoke
1 medium cooked**

Calories 64
Protein 3g
Total Fat 0g
Saturated Fat 0g
Cholesterol 0g
Carbohydrate 14g
Dietary Fiber 10g
Sodium 70mg
Potassium 340mg
Calcium 25mg
Iron 0.7mg
Vitamin A 16 IU
Vitamin C 9mg
Folate 107mcg

benefits

Artichokes are a great addition to a weight-loss plan because they are low in calories yet rich in insoluble fiber, potassium and folate. Compared to the artichoke heart, the meaty leaves contain more nutrients. Also, it takes time to eat the leaves, which helps prevent overeating by allowing the brain to realize you are full and satisfied.

selection and storage

Globe artichokes are commonly available in the produce department of the supermarket. Artichoke hearts, the meaty base, are available in cans and may be used in place of fresh in many dishes. Look for fresh artichokes with a soft green color and tightly packed, closed leaves. Store artichokes in a plastic bag in the refrigerator with a few drops of water to prevent them from drying out. Although best if used within a few days, they'll keep for a week or two if stored properly.

preparation and serving tips

Wash artichokes under running water. Pull off the lower leaves and trim off the sharp tips. Boil or steam them in a large saucepan for 20 to 40 minutes or until a center leaf pulls out easily. Artichokes can be served hot or cold. Skip the high-fat sauces and try artichokes with lemon juice and a drizzle of olive oil.

scallop and artichoke heart casserole

- 1 teaspoon canola or vegetable oil
- ¼ cup chopped red bell pepper
- ¼ cup sliced green onion tops
- ¼ cup all-purpose flour
- 2 cups low-fat (1%) milk
- 1 teaspoon dried tarragon
- ¼ teaspoon salt
- ¼ teaspoon white pepper
- 1 tablespoon chopped fresh parsley
  Dash paprika
- 1 package (9 ounces) frozen artichoke hearts, cooked
- 1 pound scallops

1. Preheat oven to 350°F. Heat oil in medium saucepan over medium-low heat. Add bell pepper and green onions; cook and stir 5 minutes or until tender. Stir in flour. Gradually whisk in milk until smooth. Add tarragon, salt and white pepper; cook and stir over medium heat 10 minutes or until sauce boils and thickens.

2. Meanwhile, cut artichoke hearts lengthwise into halves. Arrange in 8-inch square baking dish.

3. Rinse scallops; pat dry with paper towel. Cut into halves; arrange evenly over artichokes.

4. Pour sauce over scallops. Bake 25 minutes or until bubbly and scallops are opaque. Sprinkle with parsley and paprika before serving.   *Makes 4 servings*

Note: White pepper is a mild version of the common black pepper. They can be used interchangeably, although white pepper is most commonly used in light-colored foods.

nutrients per serving:

Calories 227
Calories from Fat 14%
Protein 26g
Carbohydrate 23g
Fiber 4g

Total Fat 4g
Saturated Fat 1g
Cholesterol 43mg
Sodium 438mg

Arugula

Arugula, a member of the same plant family as broccoli and cauliflower, is one of the most nutritious of all salad greens. It has a peppery mustard flavor that mixes well with other greens, but can also be eaten on its own.

benefits

Arugula is a low-calorie, nutrient-rich, flavorful vegetable, making it a great choice for dieters. It has more calcium than most other salad greens and is a good source of vitamin C, beta-carotene, iron and folate. Its cruciferous family roots means that arugula is loaded with phytonutrients, which have antioxidant power to naturally detoxify the body.

nutrients per serving:

Arugula
1 cup raw

Calories 5 **Protein** <1g **Total Fat** 0g
Saturated Fat 0g **Cholesterol** 0g
Carbohydrate 1g **Dietary Fiber** <1g
Sodium 5mg **Potassium** 70mg
Calcium 32mg **Iron** 0.3mg
Vitamin A 475 IU **Vitamin C** 3mg
Folate 19mcg

selection and storage

Arugula is often sold in small bunches with roots attached. Younger leaves, known as baby arugula, are more tender and less pungent than the more mature greens. As its popularity grows, baby arugula is likely to be found prewashed and packaged, saving the time it takes to wash away the gritty dirt that sticks to the leaves. The leaves should be bright green and fresh looking. Arugula is very perishable and should be stored tightly wrapped in the refrigerator and used within a few days.

preparation and serving tips

Arugula is a very versatile green. It goes great in mixed salads, can be substituted for basil in pesto sauces and swapped for spinach. Its oak-shaped leaves make an attractive salad dressed with olive oil, lemon juice and a few shavings of Parmesan cheese. Arugula leaves can be a lively addition to pasta dishes, soups and sautéed vegetables—just add right before serving to gently wilt the leaves.

Asparagus

You can't beat the nutrition and flavor you get for the calories from asparagus; at less than 4 calories a spear, asparagus is a winner in any weight-loss plan.

nutrients per serving:

Asparagus
½ cup cooked

Calories 20
Protein 2g
Total Fat 0g
Saturated Fat 0g
Cholesterol 0g
Carbohydrate 4g
Dietary Fiber 2g
Sodium 10mg
Potassium 200mg
Calcium 21mg
Iron 0.8mg
Vitamin A 905 IU
Vitamin C 7mg
Folate 134mcg

benefits

Asparagus is appealing to dieters because it is low in calories and high in nutrients. Two major antioxidants abundant in asparagus—beta-carotene and vitamin C—are important in the fight against heart disease and cancer. Asparagus is also a good source of potassium and folate.

selection and storage

Asparagus is first found in stores in early spring. Look for a bright green color, stalks that are smooth, firm, straight and round as well as tips that are compact, closed, pointed and purplish in color. In a bunch, choose stalks of similar size so they'll cook at the same rate. Asparagus will keep for almost a week. when wrapped loosely in a plastic bag in the vegetable drawer. To enjoy asparagus year-round, blanch the fresh spears, store them in freezer bags and freeze for up to eight months.

preparation and serving tips

Rinse asparagus thoroughly and snap off the whitish stem ends. Add these to soup stock instead of just tossing them out. Boil, steam or microwave asparagus, but avoid overcooking it. Another great cooking method is grilling or oven-roasting with a light brushing of olive oil. When cooked correctly, the spears should be crisp-tender and bright green. Overcooked spears turn mushy and a drab olive green. You can serve asparagus as a hot side dish or tossed in a cold salad. Try adding cut-up spears to your next stir-fry or pasta dish.

Bananas

Bananas are the perfect take-along snack and one of the most popular fruits in the United States.

benefits

Although higher in calories than most other fruits, bananas are fat free and high in fiber making them filling and satisfying—a great benefit when you are watching your weight. Bananas are loaded with potassium; research shows that getting enough potassium, along with weight control and a low-sodium diet, may play an important role in the control of high blood pressure. Bananas also supply vitamin C.

selection and storage

There are different types of bananas, but the classic yellow Cavendish are the most common. As bananas ripen after picking, their starch turns to sugar. So the riper they are, the sweeter they are. Look for plump, firm bananas with no bruises or split skins. Brown spots are a sign of ripening. Allow them to ripen at room temperature, refrigerating once they are ripe to stop the process. Over time, they'll turn a black color.

preparation and serving tips

Bananas are great on their own, but when mashed, they make a great low-fat, nutrient-packed spread for toasted bread or bagels. Sprinkle lemon juice on banana slices to keep them from darkening. To salvage bananas that are too ripe, peel and freeze them so you can add them to smoothies. Or use overripe bananas to make banana bread.

banana pudding squares

- 1 cup graham cracker crumbs
- 2 tablespoons margarine, melted
- 1 package (8 ounces) fat-free cream cheese, softened
- 3 cups fat-free (skim) milk
- 2 packages (4-serving size) sugar-free fat-free banana cream instant pudding and pie filling mix
- 1 container (8 ounces) reduced-fat whipped topping, divided
- 2 medium bananas

1. Line 13×9-inch baking pan with foil and spray with nonstick cooking spray. Combine graham cracker crumbs and margarine in small bowl; mix well. Spread evenly in pan.

2. Beat cream cheese in large bowl with electric mixer at low speed until smooth. Add milk and pudding mix; beat at high speed 2 minutes or until smooth and creamy. Fold half of whipped topping into pudding until well blended. Reserve half of pudding mixture. Spread remaining pudding mixture evenly onto crust.

3. Peel bananas; cut in half lengthwise, then cut crosswise into ¼-inch slices. Arrange evenly over pudding. Spread reserved pudding mixture evenly over bananas.

4. Spread remaining whipped topping evenly over pudding mixture. Loosely cover with plastic wrap and refrigerate 2 hours (or up to 8 hours) before serving.

Makes 18 servings

nutrients per serving:

Calories 112
Calories from Fat 32%
Protein 4g
Carbohydrate 15g
Fiber 1g

Total Fat 4g
Saturated Fat 2g
Cholesterol 2mg
Sodium 292mg

Barley

This flavorful grain is great for dieters because its high fiber content is quite filling, reducing the likelihood of overindulging and consuming extra calories.

benefits

Barley makes an excellent addition to a weight-loss diet—it's a healthy, carbohydrate-rich grain with plenty of fiber. Barley is rich in both soluble and insoluble fiber, helping to lower blood cholesterol levels and keep your digestive tract regular. It also provides iron.

selection and storage

Whole grain or hulled barley (unpearled) is the most nutritious, with twice the fiber, vitamins and minerals of pearl barley. Scotch barley is husked and coarsely ground. Although not the most nutritious, pearl barley is most common; it is lower in fiber because the bran has been removed, and cooks more quickly as a result. Quick barley is pearl barley that has been steamed and dried so it will cook the fastest. Store pearl and hulled barley in airtight containers in a cool, dark place.

preparation and serving tips

To cook, add 1 cup pearl barley to 2 cups boiling water (or 1 cup whole barley to 3 cups boiling water). Cover and simmer until all water is absorbed, about 10 to 15 minutes for quick barley, 45 to 55 minutes for pearl barley and 60 to 90 minutes for whole barley. You can soak whole barley overnight to reduce cooking time. As barley cooks, it swells and absorbs water, making it the perfect thickener for soups, stews and vegetarian chilis. You can also try substituting barley for rice or pasta in casserole recipes or as an accompaniment to skillet meals.

hearty mushroom barley soup

1 teaspoon extra virgin olive oil
2 cups chopped onions
1 cup thinly sliced carrots
2 cans (about 14 ounces each) fat-free
   reduced-sodium chicken broth
12 ounces sliced mushrooms
1 can (10¾ ounces) 98% fat-free cream
   of mushroom soup, undiluted
½ cup uncooked quick-cooking barley
1 teaspoon reduced-sodium
   Worcestershire sauce
½ tcaspoon dried thyme
¼ cup finely chopped green onions
¼ teaspoon salt
¼ teaspoon black pepper

1. Spray large saucepan or Dutch oven with nonstick cooking spray; heat over medium-high heat. Add oil, tilting pan to coat bottom. Add onions; cook and stir 5 minutes or until translucent. Add carrots; cook and stir 2 minutes.

2. Add broth, mushrooms, soup, barley, Worcestershire sauce and thyme; bring to a boil over high heat. Reduce heat; cover and simmer 15 minutes, stirring occasionally. Stir in green onions, salt and pepper.

Makes 4 servings

nutrients per serving:

Calories 217
Calories from Fat 18%
Protein 8g
Carbohydrate 39g
Fiber 9g
Total Fat 5g
Saturated Fat 1g
Cholesterol 0mg
Sodium 496mg

Basil

This popular herb is a member of the mint family. Its pungent flavor is a cross between licorice and cloves. Available dried or fresh, it is used abundantly in Mediterranean and Italian cooking.

benefits

Like all herbs, basil is a flavorful substitution for salt; fresh or dried basil can add satisfying flavor to low-fat foods. And fresh basil contains flavonoids and beta-carotene, powerful antioxidants that protect body cells from damage.

selection and storage

There are more than sixty varieties of basil, all of which differ in appearance and taste. The popular sweet basil has a bright, pungent taste, while other varieties like lemon basil, anise basil and cinnamon basil have subtle flavors that reflect their name. Fresh basil is available year-round in most supermarkets. Choose evenly colored leaves with no signs of wilting. Store fresh basil in the refrigerator wrapped loosely in damp paper towels in a plastic bag or with the stems in a glass of water. Use fresh basil within a week. Store dried basil in a cool, dark place for up to six months.

preparation and serving tips

Basil is well known as the main ingredient in pesto sauce, a mixture of basil, olive oil, garlic, pine nuts and Parmesan cheese. It can be used to flavor many types of foods. Be aware that the flavor and aroma of dried basil is quite different from fresh basil. When adding fresh basil to cooked dishes, add at the end of cooking to retain the most flavor and nutrients.

nutrients per serving:

Basil, fresh
¼ cup

Calories 1 **Protein** 0g **Total Fat** 0g **Saturated Fat** 0g **Cholesterol** 0g **Carbohydrate** <1g **Dietary Fiber** <1g **Sodium** 0mg **Potassium** 20mg **Calcium** 11mg **Iron** 0.2mg **Vitamin A** 316 IU **Vitamin C** 1mg **Folate** 4mcg

gazpacho pasta salad

    2 cups grape or cherry tomatoes, halved
 1⅓ cups cooked whole wheat penne
        pasta or rotini
    1 medium green bell pepper, seeded
        and chopped
    1 small cucumber, peeled and diced
    ½ cup chopped red onion
    1 tablespoon tomato juice
    1 tablespoon red wine vinegar
 1½ teaspoons olive oil
    ¼ teaspoon crushed dried oregano
    ½ teaspoon salt
    ¼ teaspoon pepper
    ¼ cup chopped fresh basil leaves

1. Combine tomatoes, pasta, bell pepper, cucumber and onion in large bowl.

2. Whisk tomato juice, vinegar, oil, oregano, salt and pepper in small bowl or cup. Pour over salad; toss to coat. Sprinkle with basil.

Makes 5 servings

nutrients per serving:

Calories 91
Calories from Fat 20%
Protein 3g
Carbohydrate 17g
Fiber 3g
Total Fat 2g
Saturated Fat <1g
Cholesterol 0mg
Sodium 248mg

Beans

What food is high in protein, low in fat and contains more fiber than most whole grains? You guessed it—beans! A food staple in many cultures for thousands of years, beans remain an important part of cuisines all around the world. There are hundreds of varieties; some are grown for their edible pods and others for their seeds, which are used either fresh or dried.

nutrients per serving:

Beans, kidney
½ cup cooked

Calories 112
Protein 8g
Total Fat 0g
Saturated Fat 0g
Cholesterol 0g
Carbohydrate 20g
Dietary Fiber 6g
Sodium 0mg
Potassium 360mg
Iron 2mg
Folate 115mcg
Magnesium 37mg
Manganese 0.4mg
Copper 0.2mg

benefits

Beans are great for dieters because they fill you up on fewer calories and contain a hefty 5 to 7 grams of fiber per ½ cup serving. Make beans the low-fat main component of your meal by substituting them for higher-fat protein sources like meats. The U.S. Dietary Guidelines recommend everyone eats 1½ cups of beans per week.

selection and storage

Beans come in a variety of shapes, colors and sizes, and are often interchangeable in recipes. They are available both dry and canned; dry beans are less expensive but require more time to prepare. Dried beans last for a year or more in an airtight container. Store cooked beans for up to one week in the refrigerator or freeze for up to six months.

preparation and serving tips

To quick soak dried beans, place them in a large saucepan and cover with 3 inches of water. Bring to a boil and boil for 2 minutes. Remove from the heat; cover and let stand for about 1 hour before proceeding with recipe directions. Salt and acidic ingredients, such as tomatoes and wine, slow down cooking and toughen beans, so add them during the last 30 minutes of cooking. Canned beans can be used in recipes in place of dry beans; be sure to drain and rinse the beans, which can reduce sodium by at least 40 percent.

white bean and chicken ragoût

- 2 boneless skinless chicken thighs
- 2 medium celery stalks, cut into ½-inch pieces
- 2 small carrots, cut into ½-inch pieces
- ¼ medium onion, chopped
- 1 clove garlic
- 1 bay leaf
- 1 sprig fresh parsley
- 1 sprig fresh thyme
- 3 black peppercorns
- 1 cup cooked cannellini beans
- 1 plum tomato, chopped
- 1 teaspoon herbes de Provence
- ½ teaspoon salt
- ⅛ teaspoon black pepper
- 1 teaspoon extra virgin olive oil
- 1 tablespoon chopped fresh parsley
- 1 teaspoon grated lemon peel

1. Place chicken in medium saucepan; add enough water to cover. Add celery, carrots, onion, garlic, bay leaf, parsley, thyme and peppercorns. Bring to a boil over high heat. Reduce heat to low; simmer 15 to 20 minutes or until vegetables are tender.

2. Remove chicken from saucepan; let cool 5 minutes. Drain vegetables; reserve broth. Discard bay leaf, parsley, garlic, thyme and peppercorns.

3. When cool enough to handle, cut chicken into bite-size pieces. Return chicken and vegetables to saucepan. Stir in beans and tomato. Add herbes de Provence, salt and black pepper. Stir in 1 cup reserved broth; simmer 5 minutes.

4. Divide between two bowls; drizzle with oil. Sprinkle with chopped parsley and lemon peel.

Makes 2 servings

nutrients per serving:

Calories 283
Calories from Fat 17%
Protein 24g
Carbohydrate 36g
Fiber 10g
Total Fat 6g
Saturated Fat <1g
Cholesterol 57mg
Sodium 715mg

Bean Sprouts

Popular in Asian cuisine, bean sprouts are the crisp, tender sprouts of a germinated mung bean. Surprisingly nutritious, bean sprouts add taste and texture to salads, stir-fries and soups.

benefits

Bean sprouts have a lot to offer for very few calories. They provide useful amounts of protein and fiber along with small amounts of a variety of vitamins and minerals. As with many sprouted foods, mung bean sprouts are higher in some nutrients than the bean itself. Bean sprouts are very low in sodium and fat free.

selection and storage

Mung bean sprouts can be purchased fresh or canned or you can try sprouting them at home. When buying fresh, look for white sprouts with a little moisture at the roots. Be aware there is a risk of foodborne illnesses if you eat raw sprouts, including *E. coli* and *Salmonella*.

Washing and chilling can reduce the risk of illness. Never eat sprouts that are slimy, brown or musty smelling. Mung bean sprouts should be refrigerated in a plastic bag and used within three days. They are also readily available in cans.

preparation and serving tips

For optimum crispness, eat fresh bean sprouts raw. Their mild flavor and delightful crunch make a nice addition to salads, sandwiches and soups. Add to stir-fries or sautéed vegetables during the last 30 seconds of cooking to help retain their texture. Canned bean sprouts can be added to various cooked dishes, but they do not have the same flavor or texture as fresh.

nutrients per serving:

Bean Sprouts, fresh ½ cup

Calories 16
Protein 2g
Total Fat 0g
Saturated Fat 0g
Cholesterol 0g
Carbohydrate 3g
Dietary Fiber 1g
Sodium 0mg
Potassium 80mg
Calcium 6mg
Iron 0.5mg
Vitamin A 11 IU
Vitamin C 7mg
Folate 32mcg

nutrients per serving:

Calories 274
Calories from Fat 26%
Protein 12g

Carbohydrate 43g
Fiber 10g
Total Fat 9g

Saturated Fat 2g
Cholesterol 3mg
Sodium 439mg

sprouts and bulgur sandwiches

½ cup bulgur wheat
1 cup water
1 container (8 ounces) plain low-fat yogurt
¼ cup fat-free salad dressing or mayonnaise
1½ teaspoons curry powder
1 cup shredded carrots
½ cup chopped apple
⅓ cup coarsely chopped peanuts
2 cups fresh bean sprouts
8 very thin slices wheat bread, toasted

1. Rinse bulgur under cold water; drain. Bring water to a boil in small saucepan over high heat. Stir in bulgur. Remove from heat. Let stand 20 minutes. Drain well.

2. Combine yogurt, salad dressing and curry in medium bowl; mix well. Stir in bulgur, carrots, apple and peanuts.

3. Arrange sprouts on four toasted bread slices. Spread with bulgur mixture and top with remaining bread slices.   *Makes 4 servings*

Beef Tenderloin

Many dieters ban beef from their weight loss plans, but there's no need to. Considered one of the 29 lean cuts of beef, this tender steak or roast contains only 8 grams of fat and 170 calories per 3-ounce serving, less than a skinless chicken thigh.

benefits

Lean beef is highly nutritious, providing high-quality protein and essential vitamins and minerals. Research shows that a diet moderately high in protein, combined with physical activity, may improve the body's ability to build muscle mass, maintain a healthy weight and curb hunger. To find other lean, protein-rich beef cuts, look for "loin" or "round" in the name.

selection and storage

Choose beef with a bright cherry-red or purplish color without any gray or brown spots. Purchase tightly sealed packages before or on the "sell by" date. Use refrigerated beef within four days after purchase or freeze immediately if you do not plan on using it right away. To keep beef tenderloin lean, trim off all visible fat.

preparation and serving tips

Tender beef cuts are best prepared with dry-heat cooking methods, such as roasting, grilling or broiling, which are great for dieters because they require little or no added fat. Add flavor by marinating 15 minutes to 2 hours or rubbing seasoning over the surface of the meat. Cook beef tenderloin to an internal temperature of at least 145°F for medium rare.

nutrients per serving:

**Beef Tenderloin, trimmed of all fat
3 ounces roasted**

Calories 174 **Protein** 23g
Total Fat 8g **Saturated Fat** 3g
Cholesterol 72g **Carbohydrate** 0g
Dietary Fiber 0g **Sodium** 50mg
Potassium 280mg **Iron** 1.4mg
Zinc 4.2mg **Phosphorus** 184mg
Vitamin B$_6$ 0.5mg **Vitamin B$_{12}$** 1.2mcg

red wine & oregano beef kabobs

¼ cup dry red wine

¼ cup finely chopped fresh parsley

2 tablespoons Worcestershire sauce

1 tablespoon reduced-sodium soy sauce

3 cloves garlic, minced

1 teaspoon dried oregano

½ teaspoon salt (optional)

½ teaspoon black pepper

¾ pound boneless beef top sirloin steak, cut into 16 (1-inch) pieces

16 whole mushrooms (about 8 ounces total)

1 medium red onion, cut into 8 wedges and separated

1. Whisk wine, parsley, Worcestershire sauce, soy sauce, garlic, oregano, salt, if desired, and pepper in small bowl. Place steak, mushrooms and onion in resealable food storage bag. Add marinade; seal bag and turn to coat. Marinate in the refrigerator 1 hour, turning frequently.

2. Meanwhile, soak four 12-inch or eight 6-inch bamboo skewers in water 20 minutes to prevent burning.

3. Spray broiler rack with cooking spray. Preheat broiler. Alternate beef, mushrooms and two layers of onion on skewers.

4. Arrange skewers on broiler rack; brush with marinade. Broil 4 to 6 inches from heat source 8 to 10 minutes, turning occasionally.

Makes 4 servings

nutrients per serving:

Calories 163
Calories from Fat 24%
Protein 22g

Carbohydrate 8g
Fiber 1g
Total Fat 4g
Saturated Fat 1g
Cholesterol 40mg
Sodium 209mg

Beets

For centuries beets were favored for their medicinal qualities, but recently they have been increasing in popularity for weight loss. Beets contain a wealth of fiber, half soluble and half insoluble, both of which have a role in successful diet plans.

nutrients per serving:

Beets
½ cup cooked

Calories 37
Protein 1g
Total Fat 0g
Saturated Fat 0g
Cholesterol 0g
Carbohydrate 8g
Dietary Fiber 2g
Sodium 65mg
Potassium 260mg
Calcium 14mg
Iron 0.7mg
Vitamin A 30 IU
Vitamin C 3mg
Folate 68mcg

benefits

Beets are a highly effective food for weight loss because they are full of nutrients and fiber while being low in calories. Beets are particularly rich in folate, fiber and potassium and their greens are full of calcium, iron, beta-carotene and vitamin C. They are also high in phytonutrients, which may help to lower cholesterol levels.

selection and storage

Choose small, firm beets that are round and uniformly sized with bright, crisp greens on top and skins that are deep red, smooth and unblemished. Remove the greens, leaving 2 inches of stem attached to prevent the beets from bleeding and the color from leaching out when cooked. Store beets and greens separately in plastic bags in the refrigerator. Beets will keep up to two weeks. They are also available canned.

preparation and serving tips

Beets can be cooked and served as a side dish, pickled for a salad or used as the main ingredient in borscht, a popular European soup. Wash beets gently as broken skin will allow color and nutrients to escape, and don't peel them before cooking for the same reason. Microwaving retains the most nutrients. Steaming is an option and takes about 25 to 45 minutes. Roast them in the oven until tender to develop their sweetness. Beet greens can be cooked and served like spinach or Swiss chard.

orange and maple glazed roasted beets

- 4 medium beets, scrubbed
- 2 teaspoons olive oil
- ¼ cup orange juice
- 3 tablespoons balsamic or cider vinegar
- 2 tablespoons maple syrup
- 2 teaspoons grated orange peel, divided
- 1 teaspoon Dijon mustard
- 1 to 2 tablespoons chopped fresh mint (optional)
- Salt and black pepper

nutrients per serving:

Calories 100
Calories from Fat 20%
Protein 2g
Carbohydrate 19g
Fiber 2g

Total Fat 3g
Saturated Fat 0g
Cholesterol 0mg
Sodium 100mg

1. Preheat oven to 425°F. Rub beets with oil; place in glass baking dish. Cover and bake 45 minutes to 1 hour or until knife inserted into largest beet goes in easily. Let stand until cool.

2. Peel beets and cut in half lengthwise; cut into wedges. Return to baking dish.

3. Whisk orange juice, vinegar, maple syrup, 1 teaspoon orange peel and mustard in small bowl until blended; pour over beets.

4. Bake 10 to 15 minutes or until heated through and liquid is absorbed. Sprinkle with remaining 1 teaspoon orange peel and mint, if desired. Season with salt and pepper.

Makes 4 servings

Bell Peppers

Bell peppers, or sweet peppers, are available in a range of colors from green to red to purple. The color indicates the degree of ripeness. They add flavor, color and crunch to many low-calorie dishes.

benefits

All bell peppers are rich in vitamins A and C, but red peppers are simply bursting with them. Volume for volume, bell peppers are higher in vitamin C than citrus fruits. Antioxidant vitamins A and C help to prevent cell damage, inflammation, cancer and diseases related to aging as well as support immune function. Lutein, an antioxidant found in bell peppers, is linked to reduced risk of macular degeneration. Bell peppers provide a decent amount of fiber, too.

selection and storage

Green peppers are red, orange or yellow peppers that haven't ripened yet. As they mature, they turn various shades until they become completely red. Once ripe, they are more perishable. Look for peppers with a glossy sheen and no shriveling, cracks or soft spots. Bell peppers should feel heavy for their size, indicating fully developed walls. Store in a plastic bag in the crisper drawer of the refrigerator. Green peppers stay firm for a week; other colors go soft within three or four days.

preparation and serving tips

Bell peppers are delicious raw in salads or as a snack with low-fat dip and are commonly incorporated into many hot dishes. They develop a stronger flavor when cooked, although they become bitter when overcooked. To roast bell peppers, preheat the broiler. Place whole peppers on a foil-covered broiler pan 4 inches from the heat source. Broil 10 to 15 minutes until blackened on all sides, turning the peppers every 5 minutes with tongs. Remove from the broiler and immediately place them in a paper bag to loosen the skin. Close the bag and set aside for 15 to 20 minutes. Peel the skin with a paring knife. Remove the cores and cut the peppers in half and rinse under cold water to remove the seeds.

nutrients per serving:

Bell Peppers, red
½ cup raw slices

Calories 14 *Protein* 1g
Total Fat 0g *Saturated Fat* 0g
Cholesterol 0g *Carbohydrate* 3g
Dietary Fiber 1g *Sodium* 0mg
Potassium 97mg *Calcium* 3mg
Iron 0.2mg *Vitamin A* 1,440 IU
Vitamin C 59mg *Folate* 21mcg

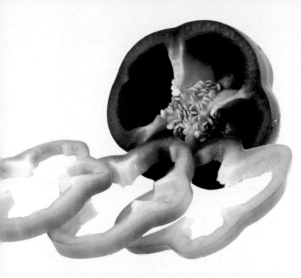

greek stuffed peppers

- 4 medium green bell peppers
- 1½ cups water, divided
- ¾ cup uncooked quick-cooking brown rice
- ½ cup grape tomatoes, quartered
- 12 pitted kalamata olives, chopped
- 3 ounces crumbled reduced-fat feta cheese
- ¼ cup chopped fresh basil
- 1 ounce pine nuts

1. Slice ¼ inch from top of peppers; remove and discard stems and seeds. Place peppers in 9-inch microwavable baking dish. Pour ¼ cup water around peppers, cover with plastic wrap and microwave on HIGH 9 to 10 minutes or until tender.

2. Meanwhile, bring remaining 1¼ cups water to a boil in medium saucepan over high heat. Add rice; reduce heat to medium-low. Cover and simmer 10 to 12 minutes or until water is absorbed and rice is tender.

3. Remove peppers from dish; drain water. Return peppers to dish, cut side up.

4. Add tomatoes, olives, feta cheese, basil and pine nuts to rice. Spoon rice mixture evenly into peppers.

Makes 4 servings

nutrients per serving:

Calories 257
Calories from Fat 35%
Protein 10g
Carbohydrate 35g
Fiber 5g

Total Fat 10g
Saturated Fat 2g
Cholesterol 6mg
Sodium 403mg

Black-Eyed Peas

Black-eyed peas are traditionally served on New Year's Day to bring good luck and prosperity in the new year. Eat them any day, however, because they're a delicious source of fiber and protein.

benefits

Black-eyed peas are a type of bean that have a distinct "black eye" in the inner curve. Black-eyed peas contain a winning combination of fiber and protein for dieters, which helps provide fullness while curbing hunger after eating. The fiber is mostly soluble, which helps lower cholesterol. Very low in fat, black-eyed peas are also the lowest in calories compared to other legumes. They provide respectable amounts of calcium, iron, potassium, and folate, too.

selection and storage

In some areas you may find fresh black-eyed peas in season but they're available everywhere year-round dried, canned and frozen. Look for dried black-eyed peas that have some shine. Choose canned black-eyed peas with no added salt or drain and rinse under cool water before using. Fresh black-eyed peas should be stored in a plastic bag in the vegetable drawer of the refrigerator and used within a week.

preparation and serving tips

Black-eyed peas can be used in soups, casseroles or served as a side dish or in the traditional New Year's Hoppin' John, which includes bacon or other high-fat ingredients, so try and use lower-fat alternatives instead. Dried black-eyed peas need to be quick-soaked or soaked overnight before cooking. Canned varieties may be too soft for some types of recipes so add them at the end of cooking.

nutrients per serving:

Black-Eyed Peas
½ cup cooked

Calories 80 *Protein* 3g *Total Fat* 0g
Saturated Fat 0g *Cholesterol* 0g
Carbohydrate 17g *Dietary Fiber* 4g
Sodium 0mg *Potassium* 345mg
Calcium 106mg *Iron* 0.9mg
Vitamin A 653 IU *Vitamin C* 2mg
Folate 105mcg

Blackberries

Sweet and juicy when fully ripe, blackberries are wonderful for both cooking and out of hand eating. Their many seeds make them high in fiber. Luckily for dieters, they are also low in calories.

benefits

With only 60 calories per 1-cup serving, you can fill up on something delightful and juicy without sabotaging your weight-loss goals. Fresh blackberries are an excellent source of vitamin C and have more fiber than a serving of some whole grain cereals. These delightful berries are packed with soluble fiber that helps slow digestion and the absorption of sugar and cholesterol.

selection and storage

Look for berries that are glossy, plump, deep-colored, firm and round. The darker the berries, the riper and sweeter they are. Refrigerate blackberries but don't wash them until you're ready to eat them because they'll get moldy. Use within a day or two after purchase as they do not last long. Try freezing washed berries in a single layer on a baking sheet. Once frozen, place them in an airtight container and thaw as needed.

preparation and serving tips

Wash blackberries gently under running water and drain well. Sort through the berries to remove stems and berries that are too soft. Do not over handle them, as their cells will break open and they will lose their juice and nutrients. Simply enjoy fresh blackberries on their own or serve them over cereal or yogurt for a sweet breakfast. Indulge and sprinkle fresh blackberries over sorbet for a divine low-fat dessert.

nutrients
per serving:

Blackberries
½ cup

Calories 31
Protein 1g
Total Fat 0g
Saturated Fat 0g
Cholesterol 0g
Carbohydrate 7g
Dietary Fiber 4g
Sodium 0mg
Potassium 120mg
Calcium 21mg
Iron 0.5mg
Vitamin A 154 IU
Vitamin C 15mg
Folate 18mcg

Blueberries

Blueberries are antioxidant superstars, delivering more than almost any other food. They are a health bargain too, providing loads of health benefits for few calories.

benefits

Antioxidants in blueberries may protect your eyes, brain cells and help reverse age-related memory loss. Besides being packed with antioxidants, blueberries are a good source of fiber and provide vitamin C and iron. Recent research suggests that when eaten as part of a healthy diet, blueberries may help reduce several risk factors for cardiovascular disease and diabetes, such as an accumulation of belly fat, high cholesterol and high blood sugar.

selection and storage

Blueberries are at their best from May through October. Choose blueberries that are firm, uniform in size and indigo blue with a silvery frost. Sort and discard shriveled or moldy berries. Do not wash until ready to use and store in a moisture-proof container in the refrigerator for up to five days. To enjoy fresh blueberries all year long, wash and dry blueberries well and freeze them in a single layer on a baking sheet. Once frozen, transfer them to a sealed bag or container.

preparation and serving tips

Enjoy blueberries' natural sweetness on cereal or yogurt, in salads or with a splash of cream. Use blueberries to make jam for a nutritious low-fat spread for toast or crackers. Frozen blueberries make a refreshing snack on a hot day and are a great addition to smoothies. Keep in mind they become mushy when thawed, if using frozen blueberries for baking. They are delicious in muffins, pancakes, quick breads, pies, cobblers and fruit crisps.

nutrients per serving:

**Blueberries
½ cup**

Calories 42
Protein 1g
Total Fat 0g
Saturated Fat 0g
Cholesterol 0g
Carbohydrate 11g
Dietary Fiber 2g
Sodium 0mg
Potassium 60mg
Calcium 4mg
Iron 0.2mg
Vitamin A 40 IU
Vitamin C 7mg
Folate 4mcg

blueberry chiffon cake

- 3 tablespoons reduced-fat margarine
- ¾ cup graham cracker crumbs
- 2 cups fresh or thawed frozen blueberries
- ½ cup cold water
- 2 envelopes unflavored gelatin
- 2 packages (8 ounces each) fat-free cream cheese
- 1 package (8 ounces) Neufchâtel cheese
- ¾ cup sugar, divided
- ⅔ cup fat-free sour cream
- ½ cup lemon juice
- 1 tablespoon grated lemon peel
- 6 egg whites*

*Use only grade A clean, uncracked eggs.

1. Preheat oven to 350°F. Melt margarine in small saucepan over medium heat. Stir in graham cracker crumbs. Press crumb mixture firmly onto bottom of 9-inch springform pan. Bake 10 minutes. Cool 10 minutes.

2. Spread blueberries in single layer in crust. Refrigerate until needed.

3. Place water in small saucepan; sprinkle gelatin over water. Let stand 3 minutes to soften. Heat gelatin mixture over low heat until completely dissolved, stirring constantly.

4. Beat cream cheese and Neufchâtel cheese in large bowl with electric mixer at medium speed until well blended. Add ½ cup sugar; beat until well blended. Add sour cream, lemon juice and lemon peel; beat until well blended. Add gelatin mixture; beat until well blended.

5. With clean, dry beaters, beat egg whites in medium bowl with electric mixer at medium speed until soft peaks form. Gradually add remaining ¼ cup sugar. Beat at high speed until stiff peaks form. Fold egg whites into cream cheese mixture. Gently spoon mixture over blueberries in prepared crust. Cover with plastic wrap. Refrigerate 6 hours or until firm.

Makes 16 servings

nutrients per serving:

Calories 165
Calories from Fat 28%
Protein 10g
Carbohydrate 20g
Fiber 1g
Total Fat 5g
Saturated Fat 2g
Cholesterol 14mg
Sodium 342mg

Broccoli

Broccoli provides more disease-fighting nutrients than most other vegetables—and for few calories.

benefits

Broccoli's noteworthy nutrients include vitamin C, vitamin A (mostly beta-carotene), folate, calcium and fiber. Broccoli is rich in an array of phytonutrients (plant nutrients) that serve as powerful cancer fighters, helping to inhibit tumor growth and boost the action of protective enzymes. Broccoli is a rich source of both soluble and insoluble fiber; soluble fiber is good for heart health while insoluble fiber helps to keep your digestive tract intact.

selection and storage

Look for broccoli that is dark green or purplish-green but not yellow; the greener the broccoli, the more beta-carotene it has. Florets should be compact and an even color, leaves should not be wilted and stalks should not be fat and woody. Store unwashed broccoli in a plastic bag in the crisper drawer of the refrigerator for a few days.

preparation and serving tips

Wash broccoli just before using. Steaming is the best way to retain its nutrients; steam 5 minutes or just until crisp-tender. Broccoli can boost the nutrition, flavor and color of any stir-fry dish. Toss raw broccoli into salads to boost the nutrition and to add bulk to the dish or serve with a low-fat dip for a great easy snack. For a low-calorie side dish, skip the cheese sauce; instead, serve with a drizzle of olive oil or squeeze of lemon and a light sprinkling of cracked pepper and sea salt.

nutrients per serving:

Broccoli
½ cup cooked

Calories 27 **Protein** 2g **Total Fat** 0g **Saturated Fat** 0g
Cholesterol 0g **Carbohydrate** 6g **Dietary Fiber** 3g
Sodium 32mg **Potassium** 229mg **Calcium** 31mg **Iron** 0.5mg
Vitamin A 1,207 IU **Vitamin C** 51mg **Folate** 84mcg

broccoli cream soup with green onions

- 1 tablespoon olive oil
- 2 cups chopped onions
- 1 pound fresh or frozen broccoli florets
- 2 cups reduced-sodium chicken or vegetable broth
- 6 tablespoons reduced-fat cream cheese
- 1 cup fat-free (skim) milk
- ¾ teaspoon salt (optional)
- ⅛ teaspoon ground red pepper
- ⅓ cup finely chopped green onions

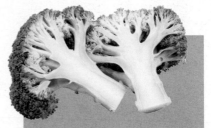

1. Heat oil in large saucepan over medium-high heat. Add onions; cook and stir 4 minutes or until translucent. Add broccoli and broth; bring to a boil. Reduce heat to medium-low; cover and simmer 10 minutes or until broccoli is tender.

2. Working in batches, process mixture in food processor or blender until smooth. Or use hand-held immersion blender. Return mixture to saucepan; heat over medium heat.

3. Whisk in cream cheese until melted. Stir in milk, salt, if desired, and red pepper; cook 2 minutes or until heated through. Top with green onions.

Makes 5 servings

nutrients per serving:

Calories 115
Calories from Fat 24%
Protein 7g
Carbohydrate 16g
Fiber 4g
Total Fat 4g
Saturated Fat 2g
Cholesterol 10mg
Sodium 569mg

Broccoli Rabe

This distant cousin of broccoli is more closely related to turnips and cabbage than broccoli. It is also known as broccoli raab or rapini. Interest in this vegetable is growing because of its nutritional benefits and savory qualities.

benefits

Like its cruciferous vegetable relatives, broccoli rabe packs a hefty dose of nutrients at a low calorie cost. Just ½ cup of broccoli rabe provides more than 10 percent of daily needs of fiber, potassium, folate and calcium and more than 50 percent of vitamins A and C. It is also loaded with cancer-fighting phytonutrients.

selection and storage

Broccoli rabe can be found from fall to spring in supermarkets with specialty produce sections. Broccoli rabe should be bright green with firm, crisp leaves, broccoli-like buds and thin stalks with no yellowing or spotting. Wrap it loosely in a plastic bag and refrigerate for up to five days. Refrigerate cooked broccoli rabe in a sealed container for up to two days.

preparation and serving tips

Broccoli rabe is a bitter green and may be an acquired taste. It has enough flavor to complement heavy spiced entrées and is a staple in Italian kitchens. If you find the flavor too strong, blanch it for 30 to 60 seconds in boiling water, then proceed with recipe directions. Remove an inch of the stems and peel the lower half, then steam or sauté until tender. Sauté in olive oil with a pinch of red pepper flakes and minced garlic for a simple side dish that allows the flavor to shine.

nutrients per serving:

Broccoli Rabe
½ cup cooked

Calories 38 **Protein** 4g
Total Fat 0.5g **Saturated Fat** 0g
Cholesterol 0g **Carbohydrate** 4g
Dietary Fiber 3g **Sodium** 64mg
Potassium 390mg **Calcium** 136mg
Iron 1.5mg **Vitamin A** 5,213 IU
Vitamin C 43mg **Folate** 82mcg

Brown Rice

Replace the white rice in your pantry with brown rice. It is more nutritious since it has a high-fiber bran coating, which gives it a light tan color. And brown rice has a nutty flavor and chewy texture that makes it a great accompaniment for many dishes.

benefits

Brown rice is a whole grain and an excellent source of complex carbohydrates. In fact, it has three times the fiber of white rice and contains more magnesium, phosphorus, manganese and selenium. Its whole grain mix of carbohydrates, fiber and protein help provide energy and a feeling of fullness that is important for weight loss. It complements meats and other proteins, particularly legumes.

selection and storage

Brown rice is more perishable than white rice but keeps for about six months, longer if refrigerated. It is available in several forms: regular (long and short grain); quick, which has been partially cooked and dehydrated; and instant, which has been fully cooked and dehydrated. The main difference in brown rice varieties is the cooking time.

preparation and serving tips

Long grain brown rice takes about 30 minutes to cook, while short grain brown rice takes about 40 minutes. Instant and quick-cooking varieties have shorter cooking times, about 10 to 15 minutes. Brown rice makes a nutritious component in stir-fries and mixed dishes with vegetables and lean meat or tofu. Try it as a cold salad with peas, red bell peppers and other vegetables dressed with a low-fat vinaigrette.

nutrients per serving:

Brown Rice, long grain
½ cup cooked

Calories 108
Protein 3g
Total Fat 1g
Saturated Fat 0g
Cholesterol 0g
Carbohydrate 22g
Dietary Fiber 2g
Sodium 5mg
Potassium 40mg
Iron 0.4mg
Magnesium 42mg
Phosphorus 81mg
Manganese 0.9mg
Selenium 9.6mcg

Brussels Sprouts

Cultivated in Belgium, these miniature vegetables are a member of the nutritious cabbage family and share many of the same health benefits.

benefits

Brussels sprouts are a good source of fiber, potassium, iron and vitamin A. They are also particularly rich in vitamin C. Brussels sprouts are naturally low in fat and calories but rather high in protein, which accounts for more than one quarter of their calories. They are so high in protein, in fact, that you can skip the higher-fat protein like meat and make them the center of your meal.

selection and storage

Fresh brussels sprouts are at their best in fall and winter. Look for a pronounced green color and tight, compact, firm heads. The fewer the yellowed, wilted or loose leaves, the better. Choose smaller heads; they're more tender and flavorful. Pick ones of similar size so they cook evenly. Stored in the refrigerator in a loosely closed plastic bag they'll last up to two weeks.

preparation and serving tips

Rinse brussels sprouts under running water, then pull off loose or wilted leaves. Trim the stem ends and cut an "X" to help them cook evenly. Steam rather than boil to preserve nutrients just until tender. Or cut them in half lengthwise, toss with olive oil, salt and pepper and roast in a 400°F oven for 20 minutes or until crisp-tender. Brussels sprouts are delicious served with just a squeeze of lemon juice or a mustard sauce.

nutrients per serving:

Brussels Sprouts
½ cup cooked

Calories 28
Protein 2g
Total Fat 0g
Saturated Fat 0g
Cholesterol 0g
Carbohydrate 6g
Dietary Fiber 2g
Sodium 15mg
Potassium 245mg
Calcium 28mg
Iron 0.9mg
Vitamin A 604 IU
Vitamin C 48mg
Folate 47mcg

autumn pasta

- **1 boneless skinless chicken breast (about ¼ pound), cut into ½-inch cubes**
- **8 brussels sprouts, trimmed and sliced**
- **1 large bulb fennel, trimmed, quartered and halved**
- **2 medium tomatoes, seeded and chopped**
- **¼ cup lemon juice**
- **1 tablespoon olive oil**
- **1 teaspoon minced garlic**
- **1 cup cooked whole grain rotini pasta**
- **2 tablespoons freshly grated Parmesan cheese**

1. Combine chicken, brussels sprouts, fennel, tomatoes, lemon juice, oil and garlic in large bowl.

2. Spray large nonstick skillet with nonstick cooking spray; heat over medium heat. Add chicken mixture; cook, covered, about 15 minutes or until vegetables are tender and chicken is cooked through.

3. Add pasta to skillet; cook until heated through. Sprinkle with Parmesan cheese.   *Makes 2 servings*

Bulgur

Bulgur, a Middle Eastern staple, is wheat kernels that have been steamed, dried and crushed. It is an inexpensive source of low-fat protein, making it a wonderfully nutritious addition to a low-calorie meal plan.

benefits

Bulgur is high in protein and minerals, making it an ideal replacement for higher-calorie protein sources like meat. Bulgur is also a standout in terms of its high fiber content. Like other wheat products, it can help keep your digestive tract healthy as well as keep you full and satisfied long after a meal.

selection and storage

Bulgur is available in three grinds—coarse, medium and fine. Coarse bulgur is used to make pilaf or stuffing. Medium-grind bulgur is used in cereals. The finest grind of bulgur is used in the popular cold Middle Eastern salad called tabbouleh. Store bulgur in an airtight container in the refrigerator; it will keep for months.

preparation and serving tips

Because bulgur is already partially cooked, little time is needed for preparation. For most types of bulgur, combine ½ cup bulgur with 1 cup boiling water. Let it stand for 10 to 15 minutes, then drain excess water and fluff with a fork. Bulgur triples in volume. If you like chewier bulgur, let it sit longer to absorb more water. Since cooking time and method vary by the coarseness of the grind, check the package for cooking instructions. Bulgur can be used in place of rice in most recipes.

nutrients per serving:

Bulgur
½ cup cooked

Calories 76
Protein 3g
Total Fat 0g
Saturated Fat 0g
Cholesterol 0mg
Carbohydrate 17g
Dietary Fiber 4g
Sodium 5mg
Potassium 60mg
Calcium 9mg
Iron 0.9mg
Vitamin A 2 IU
Vitamin C 0mg
Folate 16mcg

bulgur salad niçoise

- 2 cups water
- ¼ teaspoon salt
- 1 cup bulgur wheat
- 1 cup halved cherry tomatoes
- 1 can (6 ounces) tuna packed in water, drained and flaked
- ½ cup pitted black niçoise olives*
- 3 tablespoons finely chopped green onions
- 1 tablespoon chopped fresh mint leaves (optional)
- 1½ tablespoons lemon juice, or to taste
- 1 tablespoon olive oil
- ⅛ teaspoon black pepper
- Shredded mint leaves (optional)

*If you use larger olives, slice or chop as desired.

1. Bring water and salt to a boil in medium saucepan. Stir in bulgur; remove from heat. Cover; let stand 10 to 15 minutes or until water is absorbed and bulgur is tender. Fluff with fork; set aside to cool completely.

2. Combine bulgur, tomatoes, tuna, olives, green onions and chopped mint, if desired, in large bowl. Combine lemon juice, oil and pepper in small bowl; pour over salad. Toss gently to coat. Garnish with mint leaves, if desired.   *Makes 3 servings*

nutrients per serving:

Calories 307
Calories from Fat 23%
Protein 21g
Carbohydrate 40g
Fiber 10g
Total Fat 8g
Saturated Fat 1g
Cholesterol 17mg
Sodium 593mg

Butternut Squash

Sweet and creamy, this satisfying and fiber-rich winter squash is an excellent addition to a weight-management plan. Its tough shell allows for longer storage so you can enjoy it well into the winter and early spring months.

benefits

The fiber found in butternut squash helps you feel full and satisfied and its rich, sweet flavor doesn't need any added sugar or fat, which helps keep it low in calories. Butternut squash is bursting with beta-carotene (vitamin A), which gives it the deep orange-yellow color. This essential vitamin helps maintain eye health, promotes healthy skin and is a powerful antioxidant.

selection and storage

Butternut squash is available year-round; its peak season is from early fall through winter. It has a bulbous end, and the smooth outer shell ranges from yellow to light orange. Choose a squash that is firm and free of bruises, punctures or cuts.

Uncooked, it does not need refrigeration and can be stored in a cool, dark place for several weeks.

preparation and serving tips

The simplest way to prepare butternut squash is to cut it in half and bake or microwave it. Because the skin is so tough, use a sharp knife to cut the squash. To help soften it for easier cutting, microwave the squash for 3 to 5 minutes. Cut it in half lengthwise, then scoop out the seeds and proceed with cooking or peeling. Try a "Y" shaped vegetable peeler for best results. Add cubed squash to soups or stews or try it mashed as an alternative to sweet potatoes.

nutrients per serving:

**Butternut Squash
½ cup cooked**

Calories 41 **Protein** 1g **Total Fat** 0g
Saturated Fat 0g **Cholesterol** 0mg
Carbohydrate 11g **Dietary Fiber** 3.5g
Sodium 0mg **Potassium** 290mg
Calcium 42mg Iron 0.6mg
Vitamin A 11,434 IU **Vitamin C** 16mg
Folate 19mcg

butternut squash soup

2 teaspoons olive oil
1 large sweet onion, chopped
1 medium red bell pepper, chopped
2 packages (10 ounces each) frozen puréed
    butternut squash, thawed
1 can (10¾ ounces) condensed reduced-sodium
    chicken broth, undiluted
¼ teaspoon ground nutmeg
⅛ teaspoon white pepper
½ cup fat-free half-and-half

nutrients per serving:

Calories 152
Calories from Fat 17%
Protein 6g
Carbohydrate 28g
Fiber 3g
Total Fat 3g
Saturated Fat 1g
Cholesterol 13mg
Sodium 155mg

1. Heat oil in large saucepan over medium-high heat. Add onion and bell pepper; cook 5 minutes, stirring occasionally. Add squash, broth, nutmeg and white pepper; bring to a boil over high heat. Reduce heat to medium-low; cover and simmer 15 minutes or until vegetables are very tender.

2. Working in batches, process mixture in food processor or blender until smooth. Or use hand-held immersion blender. Return mixture to saucepan; heat over medium heat.

3. Stir in half-and-half; cook until heated through.

Makes 4 servings

Cabbage

Cabbage is truly a dieter's friend. It is fat free and has the fewest calories of any vegetable.

nutrients per serving:

Cabbage
½ cup cooked

Calories 17
Protein 1g
Total Fat 0g
Saturated Fat 0g
Cholesterol 0mg
Carbohydrate 4g
Dietary Fiber 1.5g
Sodium 6mg
Potassium 150mg
Calcium 36mg
Iron 0.1mg
Vitamin A 60 IU
Vitamin C 28mg
Folate 22mcg

benefits

Cabbage provides fiber and a respectable amount of vitamin C, potassium and folate. Savoy cabbage and bok choy also provide beta-carotene, an antioxidant that battles cancer and heart disease. Bok choy is an important source of calcium, which may help prevent osteoporosis and aid in controlling blood pressure.

selection and storage

There are hundreds of varieties of cabbage. When choosing green and red cabbage, pick a tight, compact head that looks crisp and fresh with few loose leaves. Leafy varieties should be green, with stems that are firm, not limp. Store whole heads of cabbage in the crisper drawer of the refrigerator. If uncut, compact heads keep for a couple weeks. Leafy varieties should be used within a few days.

preparation and serving tips

Discard outer leaves if loose or limp. Steam or stir-fry (in a nonaluminum pan) to preserve nutrients. Cook until crisp-tender, 10 to 12 minutes for wedges, or 5 minutes for shredded. Combine red and green cabbage for a colorful coleslaw and keep calories down by dressing it with nonfat yogurt. Bok choy and napa cabbage work well in stir-fries, while savoy is perfect for stuffing. In place of the meat in traditional stuffed cabbage recipes, try bulgur, quinoa or buckwheat.

red cabbage with apples

1 head red cabbage, shredded

2 apples, cored, peeled and thinly sliced

½ cup sliced onion

½ cup unsweetened apple juice

¼ cup lemon juice

2 tablespoons raisins

2 tablespoons brown sugar

Salt and black pepper (optional)

1. Combine cabbage, apples, onion, apple juice, lemon juice, raisins and brown sugar in large nonstick saucepan.

2. Cover and simmer over medium-low heat 30 minutes or until tender. Season with salt and pepper, if desired.   *Makes 8 servings*

nutrients per serving:

Calories 68
Calories from Fat 3%
Protein 1g
Carbohydrate 17g
Fiber 2g
Total Fat <1g
Saturated Fat <1g
Cholesterol 0mg
Sodium 13mg

Cantaloupe

It's hard to say no to melon, with its soft, sweet, juicy pulp and superb taste. That's okay because cantaloupe's nutrient-packed, juicy, sweet flesh makes a good substitute for high-calorie snacks and desserts.

benefits

Cantaloupe is great for dieters because it provides satisfying sweetness for few calories and its high water content and soluble fiber help you feel full. Cantaloupes and other yellow-orange varieties of melon are rich in vitamin C, beta-carotene and phytonutrients, a powerful trio that helps protect against heart disease, cancer and other diseases. It's also a good source of potassium, a nutrient that may help control blood pressure, regulate heart beat and possibly prevent strokes.

selection and storage

Look for cantaloupes that are evenly shaped with no bruises, cracks or soft spots. Select melons that are heavy for their size, as they tend to be juicier. Ripe cantaloupes have a mildly sweet fragrance. If the cantaloupe smells sickeningly sweet or if there is mold where the stem used to be, it is probably overripe and quite possibly rotten. Cantaloupes continue to ripen off the vine, so if you buy it ripe, eat it as soon as possible.

preparation and serving tips

Enjoy cantaloupe either slightly chilled or at room temperature for the best flavor. Chilled melon soup is a refreshing treat in hot weather. The natural cavity left in a cantaloupe after removing the seeds is a perfect place for fillers like nonfat yogurt or fruit salad. Squeeze a little lemon or lime juice onto cut melon for extra flavor.

nutrients per serving:

Cantaloupe
½ cup

Calories 27 **Protein** 1g **Total Fat** 0g
Saturated Fat 0g **Cholesterol** 0mg **Carbohydrate** 7g
Dietary Fiber 1g **Sodium** 10mg **Potassium** 210mg
Calcium 7mg **Iron** 0.2mg **Vitamin A** 2,706 IU
Vitamin C 29mg **Folate** 17mcg

fruit salad with cherry vinaigrette

3 cups diced cantaloupe
1 large mango, peeled and diced
¼ cup sliced almonds
½ cup fresh cherries, pitted and chopped
¼ cup orange juice
2 tablespoons balsamic vinegar
1 tablespoon honey
1 tablespoon canola oil
Pinch of salt

1. Combine cantaloupe and mango in large bowl.

2. Whisk cherries, orange juice, vinegar, honey, oil and salt in small bowl. Pour over fruit; toss to coat. Sprinkle with almonds.   *Makes 8 servings*

Variation: Substitute peaches or nectarines for the mango. If fresh cherries aren't available, use frozen cherries that have been thawed and drained well.

nutrients per serving:

Calories 75
Calories from Fat 22%
Protein <1g
Carbohydrate 15g
Fiber 1g
Total Fat 2g
Saturated Fat <1g
Cholesterol 0mg
Sodium 11mg

Carrots

When eaten with a meal, carrots help fill you up, leaving less room for higher-calorie foods. They are very versatile and can be used in soups, sauces, casseroles and quick breads.

nutrients per serving:

Carrots
½ cup raw

Calories 25
Protein 1g
Total Fat 0g
Saturated Fat 0g
Cholesterol 0mg
Carbohydrate 6g
Dietary Fiber 2g
Sodium 40mg
Potassium 195mg
Calcium 20mg
Iron 0.2mg
Vitamin A 10,191 IU
Vitamin C 4mg
Folate 12mcg

benefits

Carrots have few rivals when it comes to beta-carotene—a mere ½ cup packs a whopping amount. This type of vitamin A is good for your eyes, preventing night blindness and helping ward off cataracts. The soluble fiber in carrots helps lower blood cholesterol levels and fight hunger.

selection and storage

Look for firm carrots with bright orange color and smooth skin. Avoid those that are limp or black near the tops; they're not fresh. Choose medium-size carrots that taper at the ends; thicker ones may be tough. In general, early carrots are more tender but less sweet than larger, mature carrots. Baby carrots are sweet and provide all the nutrients with extra convenience. Carrots keep for a few weeks in the refrigerator.

preparation and serving tips

Thoroughly wash and scrub whole carrots to remove soil contaminants. To remove pesticide residues, peel the outer layer and cut off the stem end. Carrots are a great raw snack, of course, but their true sweet flavor shines through when cooked. Very little nutritional value is lost in cooking. In fact, the nutrients in lightly steamed carrots are more usable by your body than those in raw carrots.

carrot and oat muffins

½ cup fat-free (skim) milk
½ cup unsweetened applesauce
2 eggs, beaten
1 tablespoon canola oil
½ cup shredded carrot (1 large carrot)
1 cup minus 2 tablespoons
   old-fashioned oats
¾ cup whole wheat flour
¾ cup all-purpose flour
⅓ cup sugar
1½ teaspoons baking powder
1 teaspoon ground cinnamon
½ teaspoon baking soda
¼ teaspoon salt
¼ cup finely chopped walnuts (optional)

1. Preheat oven to 350°F. Spray 12 standard (2½-inch) muffin cups with nonstick cooking spray.

2. Beat milk, applesauce, eggs and oil in large bowl. Stir in carrot. Combine oats, whole wheat flour, all-purpose flour, sugar, baking powder, cinnamon, baking soda and salt in large bowl; mix well. Add to applesauce mixture; stir until batter is just moistened.

3. Spoon batter into prepared muffin cups, filling two-thirds full. Sprinkle 1 teaspoon walnuts over each muffin, if desired. Bake 20 to 22 minutes or until muffins are golden brown. Cool in pan 5 minutes. Remove to wire rack to cool completely.

Makes 12 servings

nutrients per serving:

Calories 130
Calories from Fat 18%
Protein 3g
Carbohydrate 23g
Fiber 2g
Total Fat 3g
Saturated Fat <1g
Cholesterol 35mg
Sodium 182mg

Cauliflower

Cauliflower, one of several cruciferous vegetables, is more nutritious than its colorless appearance would lead you to believe. Filling, high in fiber and low in calories, this is an ideal vegetable to include in a weight-management plan.

benefits

Raw cauliflower makes a wonderful snack for dieters. Because it is extra crunchy, cauliflower takes longer to chew, giving your body time to realize you're full. After citrus fruits, cauliflower is your next best natural source of vitamin C and is also notable for its fiber, folate and potassium content. Cauliflower also contains a type of phytonutrient called indoles that may stimulate enzymes that block cancer growth.

selection and storage

Though cauliflower is available year-round, it is more reasonably priced in fall and winter. Look for creamy white heads with compact florets. Brown patches and opened florets are signs of age. Store unwashed, uncut cauliflower loosely wrapped in a plastic bag in the crisper drawer of the refrigerator for two to five days.

preparation and serving tips

Remove the outer leaves, break off florets, trim brown spots and wash under cool running water before using. Cauliflower serves up well both raw and cooked; its flavor is less intense raw. Steam, roast, sauté or microwave cauliflower, but don't overcook it; overcooking destroys its vitamin C and folate contents. Although cheese sauces are a popular accompaniment to cauliflower, skip them because they add fat and calories. Instead, try serving it with some snipped fresh dill and a drizzle of olive oil. For a mashed potato swap, mash cooked cauliflower with olive oil, garlic and milk.

nutrients per serving:

Cauliflower
½ cup cooked

Calories 14 *Protein* 1g *Total Fat* 0g *Saturated Fat* 0g
Cholesterol 0mg *Carbohydrate* 3g *Dietary Fiber* 1.5g
Sodium 10mg *Potassium* 90mg *Calcium* 10mg *Iron* 0.2mg
Vitamin A 7 IU *Vitamin C* 28mg *Folate* 27mcg

barley vegetable casserole

2¼ cups vegetable broth, divided
⅔ cup uncooked pearl barley
4 cups frozen or fresh mixed vegetables (broccoli, cauliflower, carrots and onions)
½ teaspoon garlic powder
¼ teaspoon black pepper
½ teaspoon margarine
½ teaspoon salt (optional)

1. Preheat oven to 350°F. Spray 1-quart casserole with nonstick cooking spray.

2. Combine ¼ cup broth and barley in nonstick skillet; cook and stir over medium heat 3 minutes or until lightly browned. Transfer to prepared casserole.

3. Add mixed vegetables, garlic powder, pepper and remaining 2 cups broth; mix well.

4. Cover and bake 50 minutes or until barley is tender and most liquid is absorbed, stirring several times during baking. Stir in margarine and salt, if desired. Let stand 5 minutes before serving. *Makes 4 servings*

nutrients per serving:

Calories 155
Calories from Fat 9%
Protein 5g
Carbohydrate 30g
Fiber 8g
Total Fat 1g
Saturated Fat 0g
Cholesterol 0mg
Sodium 298mg

Celery

It is often said that celery has negative calories because chewing it burns more calories than it provides. Whether or not that's true, its low calorie count makes it worth adding to your diet.

nutrients per serving:

Celery
½ cup raw

Calories 8
Protein 0g
Total Fat 0g
Saturated Fat 0g
Cholesterol 0mg
Carbohydrate 2g
Dietary Fiber 1g
Sodium 40mg
Potassium 130mg
Calcium 20mg
Iron 0.1mg
Vitamin A 227 IU
Vitamin C 2mg
Folate 18mcg

benefits

Celery is about 95 percent water by weight and it's very low in calories—about 10 calories per serving. The high amount of water and fiber content make celery filling and satisfying to munch on. Celery is a decent source of potassium and also contains good amounts of vitamin C and folate. Celery leaves are the most nutritious part of the plant, containing more calcium, iron, potassium, beta-carotene and vitamin C than the stalks.

selection and storage

Choose firm bunches of celery that are tightly formed; the leaves should be green and crisp. Store celery in a plastic bag in the refrigerator up to two weeks, leaving the ribs attached to the stalk until ready to use. Precut celery is also available, although it will not last as long.

preparation and serving tips

Separate celery stalks and rinse well to remove dirt from the inner stalk. Remove the leaves and reserve for soups and salads. When serving celery raw, you can use a peeler to remove the outer threads. Pair raw celery with a low-fat dip or fill the stalk with peanut butter or cream cheese for a protein-packed snack. Sautéed celery and onions (mirepoix) make a delicious base for soups, stews and casseroles.

quick turkey pot pie

Filling

    2 teaspoons olive oil
    1 cup diced red bell pepper
    2 stalks celery, sliced
    1 small onion, chopped
    2 tablespoons all-purpose flour
 1¼ cups fat-free reduced-sodium
        chicken broth
    1 cup cubed peeled potato
  ½ teaspoon dried thyme
  ¼ teaspoon salt
  ¼ teaspoon black pepper
    2 cups cubed cooked turkey
        breast (about 10 ounces)
  ⅓ cup frozen peas

Biscuit Topping

  ¾ cup all-purpose flour
  ¾ teaspoon baking powder
  ⅛ teaspoon salt
  ⅛ teaspoon baking soda
    3 tablespoons cold reduced-fat
        stick margarine, cubed
    3 to 5 tablespoons buttermilk

1. Preheat oven to 425°F. Heat oil in large skillet over medium heat. Add bell pepper, celery and onion; cook and stir 4 to 5 minutes. Stir in flour until blended. Add broth, potato, thyme, salt and black pepper; bring to a boil. Reduce heat to medium-low; cover and simmer 8 to 10 minutes.

2. Add turkey and peas; simmer 5 to 7 minutes or until potato is tender and peas are heated through. Pour into 1½-quart casserole.

3. Combine flour, baking powder, salt and baking soda in medium bowl. Cut in margarine with pastry blender or two knives until mixture resembles coarse crumbs. Stir in buttermilk, 1 tablespoon at a time, until dough forms. Place on floured surface; knead lightly. Pat out to ½-inch thickness.

4. Cut dough into five biscuits with 2-inch biscuit cutter, rerolling dough as needed. Place on top of filling. Bake 12 to 14 minutes or until filling is hot and biscuits are lightly browned

Makes 5 servings

Cheese

Any way you slice it, cheese adds flavor and richness to any meal. Even a small amount of cheese can liven up low-calorie dishes.

benefits

Cheese is a concentrated source of many of the nutrients found in milk, including calcium, protein, phosphorus, magnesium, potassium, vitamin A, riboflavin and vitamin B_{12}. A 1-ounce serving of most types of cheese is equivalent to one serving of high-quality protein, which makes cheese a satisfying food that staves off hunger. One serving also typically contains 20 percent of the recommended daily intake of calcium. As an added bonus, cheese fights tooth decay by helping to protect teeth from cavity-causing bacteria.

selection and storage

There are hundreds of varieties of cheese, some of which are available in various flavors. Look for cheese in reduced-fat or part-skim varieties to save on calories and fat. Purchase cheese by the "sell-by" date and store tightly wrapped in the cheese compartment of the refrigerator for several weeks.

preparation and serving tips

Cheese can be eaten alone as a snack or added to other dishes. When paired with fruits, vegetables and whole grains, cheese boosts the nutrition and flavor of other foods. Hard cheeses such as Parmesan and Asiago and aromatic, sharp cheeses such as sharp Cheddar and Gorgonzola are so flavorful that you can add less, saving calories while still getting delicious cheesy taste.

nutrients per serving:

**Cheese, reduced-fat provolone
1 ounce**

Calories 77
Protein 7g
Total Fat 5g
Saturated Fat 3g
Cholesterol 15mg
Carbohydrate 1g
Dietary Fiber 0g
Sodium 245mg
Potassium 39mg
Calcium 212mg
Iron 0.2mg
Vitamin A 149 IU
Phosphorus 139mg
Vitamin B_{12} 0.4mcg

nutrients per serving:

**Cheese, Cheddar
1 ounce**

Calories 114 *Protein* 7g *Total Fat* 9g *Saturated Fat* 6g *Cholesterol* 30mg *Carbohydrate* 0.5g *Dietary Fiber* 0g *Sodium* 176mg *Potassium* 28mg *Calcium* 204mg *Iron* 0.2mg *Vitamin A* 284 IU *Phosphorus* 145mg *Vitamin B_{12}* 0.3mcg

black bean quesadillas

Nonstick cooking spray
4 (8-inch) flour tortillas
¾ cup (3 ounces) shredded reduced-fat Monterey Jack or Cheddar cheese
½ cup canned black beans, rinsed and drained
2 green onions, sliced
¼ cup chopped fresh cilantro
½ teaspoon ground cumin
½ cup salsa
2 tablespoons plus 2 teaspoons fat-free sour cream
Additional fresh cilantro (optional)

1. Preheat oven to 450°F. Spray large nonstick baking sheet with cooking spray. Place two tortillas on prepared baking sheet; sprinkle each with half the cheese.

2. Combine beans, green onions, cilantro and cumin in small bowl. Spoon evenly over cheese; top with remaining two tortillas. Spray tops of tortillas with cooking spray.

3. Bake 10 to 12 minutes or until cheese is melted and tortillas are lightly browned. Cut into quarters; top each tortilla wedge with 1 tablespoon salsa and 1 teaspoon sour cream. Garnish with cilantro.   *Makes 8 servings*

Note: These quesadillas are great as an afternoon snack or as an appetizer.

nutrients per serving:

Calories 105
Calories from Fat 34%
Protein 7g
Carbohydrate 13g
Fiber 1g

Total Fat 4g
Saturated Fat 1g
Cholesterol 8mg
Sodium 259mg

Chicken Breasts

Without the skin, chicken breasts are one of the leanest meats you will find. A versatile source of high-quality protein, chicken breasts contain significantly less saturated fat than other types of meat.

benefits

Chicken breasts have less fat than any other chicken part. Removing the skin makes them more diet-friendly—you will save about 60 calories, 4 grams of fat and 1 gram of saturated fat. Chicken is a good source of several B vitamins that are important for healthy metabolism and immune function, including vitamins B6, B12 and niacin.

selection and storage

Chicken breasts are available in various forms; whole breasts with the skin on are the most economical but for convenience, choose boneless skinless chicken breasts. Avoid preseasoned chicken breasts, which can be high in sodium. Refrigerate raw chicken for up to two days and cooked chicken up to three days. When freezing raw chicken, seal tightly in a plastic bag to prevent freezer burn and use within two months.

preparation and serving tips

To help chicken breasts stay lean, use a low-fat cooking method such as baking, roasting, grilling, broiling or stewing. It makes little difference whether the skin is removed before or after cooking, but the meat is more moist and tender when cooked with the skin. Cook until the internal temperature is 165°F. Boneless chicken will cook faster than bone-in—just avoid overcooking which will make it dry and tough.

nutrients per serving:

**Chicken Breast, skinless
3 ounces roasted**

Calories 140 *Protein* 26g *Total Fat* 3g *Saturated Fat* 1g
Cholesterol 72mg *Carbohydrate* 0g *Dietary Fiber* 0g
Sodium 60mg *Potassium* 220mg *Iron* 0.9mg *Vitamin B6* 0.5mg
Vitamin B12 0.3mcg *Niacin* 12mcg

chicken nuggets with barbecue dipping sauce

¼ **cup all-purpose flour**
¼ **teaspoon salt**
   Dash black pepper
2 **cups crushed reduced-fat baked cheese crackers**
1 **teaspoon dried oregano**
1 **egg white**
1 **tablespoon water**
1 **pound boneless skinless chicken breasts, cut into 1-inch pieces**
3 **tablespoons barbecue sauce**
2 **tablespoons no-sugar-added peach or apricot fruit spread**

1. Preheat oven to 400°F. Place flour, salt and pepper in large resealable food storage bag. Combine crushed crackers and oregano in shallow bowl. Whisk egg white and water in small bowl.

2. Place six to eight chicken pieces in bag with flour mixture; seal bag. Shake until chicken is well coated. Remove chicken from bag; shake off excess flour. Coat all sides of chicken pieces with egg white mixture. Roll in crumb mixture. Place in shallow baking pan. Repeat with remaining chicken pieces. Bake 10 to 13 minutes or until golden brown.

3. Meanwhile, combine barbecue sauce and fruit spread in small saucepan; cook and stir over low heat until heated through. Serve chicken nuggets with dipping sauce.

Makes 8 servings

nutrients per serving:

Calories 167
Calories from Fat 22%
Protein 14g
Carbohydrate 16g
Fiber <1g
Total Fat 4g
Saturated Fat 1g
Cholesterol 61mg
Sodium 313mg

Chile Peppers

Ranging from mild to very hot, chile peppers add a ton of spice and flavor to many foods. Emerging research suggests these little veggies are also great for helping manage your weight.

benefits

Capsaicin, the substance in chile peppers that gives them their characteristic bite, may help rev up your metabolism and work as an appetite suppressant. Using chile peppers is an easy, low-calorie way to spice up any bland food but go easy on hot peppers if you have a sensitive stomach. Chile peppers are rich in the antioxidants beta-carotene and vitamin C, both important in the fight against heart disease.

selection and storage

Choose chile peppers based on the heat they provide. Mild to moderately hot chiles include Anaheim, ancho and poblano peppers; hotter varieties include cayenne, jalapeño, serrano and habanero. Fresh chile peppers should have a deep, vivid color with no shriveling. Store peppers in the vegetable drawer of the refrigerator. Chiles are available dried, both whole and in flakes, and as pastes, hot sauces and powders.

preparation and serving tips

To cool the fire of hot peppers, cut away the inside white membrane and discard the seeds. Wash hands, utensils and cutting boards with soap and water after handling them and use gloves to prevent the oils from irritating your hands. Avoid touching your eyes while handling peppers, and even for awhile after. Chile peppers can be used in many types of dishes, especially in southwestern, Mexican and Asian cooking. Dried chile flakes are an easy way to add spice to pizza, salads, soups and chili.

nutrients per serving:

Chile Peppers, red 2 tablespoons raw chopped

Calories 8
Protein 0g
Total Fat 0g
Saturated Fat 0g
Cholesterol 0mg
Carbohydrate 2g
Dietary Fiber <1g
Sodium 0mg
Potassium 60mg
Calcium 3mg
Iron 0.2mg
Vitamin A 178 IU
Vitamin C 27mg
Folate 4mcg

vietnamese beef and noodle soup

4 cups water
2 ounces whole wheat angel hair pasta, broken in half
2¼ cups fat-free reduced-sodium beef stock
1 shallot, sliced
1 whole star anise
½ teaspoon minced fresh ginger
1 teaspoon fish sauce
1 teaspoon reduced-sodium soy sauce
½ teaspoon hot pepper sauce
6 ounces boneless beef sirloin, sliced ⅛ inch thick
⅛ teaspoon salt
⅛ teaspoon black pepper
1 cup bean sprouts
2 green onions, thinly sliced
1 small fresh red chile pepper, thinly sliced
2 tablespoons fresh cilantro leaves
2 lime wedges

1. Bring water to a boil in small saucepan. Add pasta; cook 3 to 4 minutes or until tender. Drain; set aside.

2. Bring stock, shallot, star anise and ginger to a boil in medium saucepan. Reduce heat to medium-low; simmer 10 minutes. Strain liquid into large saucepan; discard solids. Stir in fish sauce, soy sauce and hot pepper sauce.

3. Season beef with salt and pepper. Add beef and bean sprouts to stock mixture; cook 1 to 2 minutes or until beef is no longer pink. Stir in cooked pasta and green onions.

4. Top each serving with chile slices and cilantro. Drizzle with lime juice.

Makes 2 servings

nutrients per serving:

Calories 258
Calories from Fat 21%
Protein 23g
Carbohydrate 27g
Fiber 5g
Total Fat 6g
Saturated Fat 2g
Cholesterol 40mg
Sodium 515mg

Cocoa

Naturally unsweetened and nearly fat free, cocoa powder adds wonderful chocolate taste, as well as health benefits, to low-calorie foods. This rich and flavorful powder is made by removing much of the fat, or cocoa butter, from the cocoa bean.

nutrients per serving:

Cocoa Powder
1 tablespoon

Calories 12
Protein 1g
Total Fat 0.5g
Saturated Fat 0g
Cholesterol 0mg
Carbohydrate 3g
Dietary Fiber 2g
Sodium 0mg
Potassium 82mg
Calcium 7mg
Iron 0.8mg
Magnesium 27mg
Phosphorus 40mg
Copper 0.2mg

benefits

Cocoa powder is a concentrated source of plant nutrients called polyphenols, as well as minerals including iron, magnesium, phosphorus, potassium and copper. Its antioxidant properties may help prevent cancer and heart disease. Cocoa powder provides fiber, about 2 grams per tablespoon, and a small amount of protein.

selection and storage

Natural cocoa powder has a light brown color and is quite acidic, giving it a more intense and bitter flavor. Alkalized cocoa powder, or Dutch process, has been treated to lower the acidity and has a darker color and milder flavor. Keep cocoa powder in an opaque, airtight container in a cool, dark place; it will last up to two years. Don't mistake cocoa powder for hot cocoa mix, which blends cocoa powder with powdered milk and sugar and is not appropriate for baking.

preparation and serving tips

Cocoa powder is most often used in baked goods, such as brownies and cakes, or in low-fat puddings and beverages. When baking with cocoa powder, keep in mind that natural cocoa can create the rise in batter due to its high acid content, while Dutch process cocoa needs baking powder to create the same effect. Cocoa powder can also be used in savory foods, such as Mexican mole sauce, and is often the secret ingredient in chilis.

cocoa chewies

⅓ **cup powdered sugar**
2 **tablespoons flaked coconut**
2 **tablespoons unsweetened cocoa powder**
1 **tablespoon cornstarch**
3 **egg whites**
½ **teaspoon vanilla**
¼ **cup granulated sugar**

1. Preheat oven to 250°F. Line baking sheets with parchment paper or foil.

2. Combine powdered sugar, coconut, cocoa powder and cornstarch in small bowl. Beat egg whites and vanilla in medium bowl with electric mixer at high speed until foamy. Gradually add granulated sugar, 1 tablespoon at a time, beating until stiff peaks form. Gently fold in coconut mixture.

3. Pipe or spoon mixture into scant 2-inch stars or mounds on prepared baking sheets. Bake 1 hour. Cool cookies completely on baking sheets.

Makes 12 servings (2 cookies per serving)

nutrients per serving:

Calories 42
Calories from Fat 0%
Protein 1g
Carbohydrate 9g
Fiber <1g
Total Fat 0g
Saturated Fat <1g
Cholesterol 0mg
Sodium 14mg

Coffee

Coffee is prized for its strong aroma, rich flavor and the caffeine buzz it provides. It is also loved by dieters because it is nearly calorie free and may boost weight-loss efforts.

benefits

Research suggests that caffeine may support weight-loss efforts by temporarily suppressing appetite as well as increasing the number of calories burned during digestion. These effects are quite small, however, and the research is far from definitive. Coffee also helps fill you up and prevent you from overeating. Caffeine is a stimulant, and too much of it can cause nervousness, insomnia and other problems, so limit your intake to no more than 3 cups per day (or about 300 milligrams of caffeine).

selection and storage

You'll find several coffee selections in the grocery store, from whole to ground to instant, mild to full-bodied and flavored. Choose any form and flavor you prefer. Store coffee beans or grounds in an airtight container in a cool, dry place. Freeze coffee beans that you won't use within a week or ground coffee that you won't use within a few days.

preparation and serving tips

Enjoy your coffee with minimal added sugar and fat. Beware of coffee drinks loaded with sugary syrups, whole milk and whipped cream, which can add loads of calories and fat. Coffee also adds flavor and depth to various recipes, from desserts to main dishes such as chilis, pasta sauces or in marinades and glazes for meats.

nutrients per serving:

Coffee
1 cup brewed

Calories 2 *Protein* 0g *Total Fat* 0g *Saturated Fat* 0g
Cholesterol 0mg *Carbohydrate* 0g *Dietary Fiber* 0g
Sodium 5mg *Potassium* 115mg *Calcium* 5mg *Iron* 0mg
Vitamin A 0 IU *Vitamin C* 0mg *Folate* 5mcg

iced cappuccino

1 cup fat-free vanilla frozen
   yogurt or fat-free vanilla
   ice cream
1 cup cold strong brewed coffee
1 packet sugar substitute *or*
   2 teaspoons sugar
1 teaspoon unsweetened
   cocoa powder
1 teaspoon vanilla

1. Place all ingredients in food processor or blender; process until smooth. Freeze 1½ to 2 hours or until top and sides of mixture are partially frozen.

2. Process mixture again in food processor or blender until smooth and frothy. Serve immediately.

Makes 2 servings

Iced Mocha Cappuccino: Increase cocoa to 1 tablespoon. Proceed as directed above.

Tip: To add an extra flavor boost to this refreshing drink, add orange peel, lemon peel or a dash of ground cinnamon to your coffee grounds before brewing.

Corn

Enjoy these sweet kernels of goodness fresh from the cob, from a can, cooked frozen or popped. Make corn a regular part of your diet to help fill you up and curb your appetite, making it easier to lose weight.

benefits

Corn is a low-fat complex carbohydrate that is hearty and satisfying. It is high in fiber and contains a lot of water, creating a feeling of fullness from fewer calories. Plain popcorn is a delicious snack that's naturally low in calories and fat. Plus you can have a large volume for a small amount of calories.

selection and storage

When buying sweet corn, be sure it is truly fresh. Once corn is picked, the natural sugar begins turning to starch and the corn loses some sweetness. Corn is best eaten within a day or two of picking. Once home, refrigerate corn immediately. Sweet corn is also available frozen and canned; keep it healthy by avoiding butter and creamy sauces. Buy popcorn kernels to pop yourself on the stovetop or in an air popper or look for low-fat microwave popcorn.

preparation and serving tips

Boiling is the traditional method for preparing corn on the cob, though grilling, steaming and even microwaving work great, too. Overcooking toughens kernels, so cook for the shortest amount of time possible. Skip the butter and simply season with fresh herbs, lemon juice, salt and pepper. For a Southwestern flavor, try rubbing sweet corn with a lime wedge and sprinkle lightly with chili powder.

nutrients per serving:

Corn
½ cup cooked

Calories 72 **Protein** 3g **Total Fat** 1g
Saturated Fat 0g **Cholesterol** 0mg
Carbohydrate 16g **Dietary Fiber** 2g
Sodium 0mg **Potassium** 160mg
Calcium 2mg **Iron** 0.3mg
Vitamin A 196 IU **Vitamin C** 4mg
Folate 17mcg

charred corn salad

4 to 6 ears corn, husked
⅔ cup canned black beans, rinsed
 and drained
½ cup chopped fresh cilantro
2 teaspoons minced seeded chipotle
 pepper (1 canned pepper in
 adobo sauce *or* 1 dried pepper,
 reconstituted in boiling water)
3 tablespoons fresh lime juice
½ teaspoon salt
¼ cup extra virgin olive oil

1. Heat large skillet over medium-high heat. Add corn; cook in single layer 15 to 17 minutes or until browned and tender, turning frequently.

2. Remove from heat; let stand until cool enough to handle. Slice kernels off ears and place in medium bowl.

3. Place beans in small microwavable bowl; microwave on HIGH 1 minute or until heated through. Add to corn. Stir in cilantro and chipotle pepper..

4. Whisk lime juice and salt in small bowl. Gradually whisk in oil. Pour over corn mixture; toss to coat.

Makes 6 servings

nutrients per serving:

Calories 150
Calories from Fat 9%
Protein 5g
Carbohydrate 29g
Fiber 4g
Total Fat 1g
Saturated Fat <1g
Cholesterol 0mg
Sodium 285mg

Cottage Cheese

Many fad diets tout cottage cheese as a miracle food but there's no magic to it; low-fat cottage cheese is simply a good choice for dieters because it offers filling high-quality protein.

benefits

Cottage cheese is low in carbohydrates, relatively high in protein and can be low in fat, making it a good choice for dieters. It provides long-lasting energy, so you won't feel the need to snack as often. Accompanied by fresh fruit or vegetables, cottage cheese becomes the center of a nutrient-rich, appetite-curbing meal. Cottage cheese also provides calcium and other nutrients found in milk, but in lower amounts.

selection and storage

Choose low-fat (1%) or fat-free cottage cheese for less calories and fat than whole milk (4%) cottage cheese. It comes in a small, medium or large curd, which does not affect its nutrition profile. Cottage cheese is also available flavored, such as with chives or pineapple, or you can add your own favorite ingredients. Cottage cheese is perishable and must be stored in the refrigerator.

preparation and serving tips

The flavor of cottage cheese pairs well with fresh vegetables and fruits such as tomatoes, peppers, pineapple, peaches and berries. Low-fat or fat-free cottage cheese is also a useful ingredient in various recipes. Use it to replace higher-fat cream cheese in desserts like cheesecake, or in dips and sauces. Use it in pasta dishes like lasagna or stuffed shells and in egg-based dishes like quiche or frittatas to replace higher-fat cheeses.

nutrients per serving:

Cottage Cheese, low-fat (1%)
½ cup

Calories 81
Protein 14g
Total Fat 1g
Saturated Fat 0.5g
Cholesterol 5mg
Carbohydrate 3g
Dietary Fiber 0g
Sodium 460mg
Potassium 95mg
Calcium 69mg
Iron 0.2mg
Vitamin A 46 IU
Vitamin C 0mg
Folate 14mcg

cottage cheese breakfast parfaits

1 cup halved green or red
   seedless grapes
1 cup sliced strawberries
½ cup diced cantaloupe cubes
½ cup diced honeydew cubes
1 container (16 ounces) low-fat
   (1%) cottage cheese
¼ cup toasted sliced almonds*
Ground nutmeg (optional)

To toast almonds, place in small dry skillet. Cook over medium heat 1 to 2 minutes or until almonds are lightly browned, stirring constantly.

1. Combine grapes, strawberries, cantaloupe and honeydew.

2. Layer half of cottage cheese in four glasses; top with half of fruit and half of almonds. Repeat layers. Sprinkle with nutmeg, if desired.
Makes 4 servings

Note: Serve these parfaits immediately. Making them too far in advance will cause the melon to weep into the cottage cheese.

Cucumber

Be cool as a cucumber by adding cucumbers to your diet! With bright green skin, crisp refreshing flesh and tender seeds, they're a delicious and juicy food to add to your weight-loss plan.

nutrients per serving:

Cucumber
½ cup raw

Calories 8
Protein 0g
Total Fat 0g
Saturated Fat 0g
Cholesterol 0mg
Carbohydrate 2g
Dietary Fiber <1g
Sodium 0mg
Potassium 75mg
Calcium 8mg
Iron 0.2mg
Vitamin A 55 IU
Vitamin C 2mg
Folate 4mcg

benefits

Cucumbers are approximately 95 percent water, which adds a ton of volume and bulk to meals to help fill you up for very few calories.

selection and storage

Cucumbers are available year-round. Choose firm cucumbers with smooth, bright skins. If you plan to eat the seeds, avoid larger cucumbers; as cucumbers mature, the seeds grow larger and become bitter tasting. Smaller cucumber varieties are used to make pickles. Store unwashed cucumbers in a plastic bag in the refrigerator for up to ten days. Cut cucumbers can be refrigerated tightly wrapped for up to five days.

preparation and serving tips

Wash cucumbers thoroughly just before using. Supermarket cucumbers are covered with an edible wax to protect them from moisture loss. If you prefer not to eat the wax you can peel the cucumber or use a produce rinse to help remove it. Sliced cucumbers can be eaten as a refreshing snack with a low-fat dip or added to tossed salads or sandwiches. Try an Indian-inspired salad with cucumbers, fresh herbs and plain yogurt. Cucumber is also excellent in a low-calorie cold soup. Try pickling your own cucumbers for a crisp and refreshing snack or condiment.

summer's best gazpacho

- 3 cups reduced-sodium tomato juice
- 2½ cups finely diced tomatoes (about 2 large)
- 1 cup finely diced yellow or red bell pepper (about 1 small)
- 1 cup finely diced unpeeled cucumber
- ½ cup chunky salsa
- 1 tablespoon olive oil
- 1 clove garlic, minced
- 1 ripe avocado, diced
- ¼ cup finely chopped fresh cilantro or basil

1. Combine tomato juice, tomatoes, bell pepper, cucumber, salsa, oil and garlic in large bowl; mix well. Cover and refrigerate at least 1 hour or up to 24 hours before serving.

2. Stir in avocado and cilantro just before serving.   *Makes 6 servings*

nutrients per serving:

Calories 127
Calories from Fat 57%
Protein 4g
Carbohydrate 15g
Fiber 4g
Total Fat 8g
Saturated Fat 1g
Cholesterol 0mg
Sodium 444mg

Dark Chocolate

While it may seem too good to be true, it isn't—chocolate can be a part of your diet! Small amounts of chocolate may actually support weight-loss goals by reducing cravings so you can stick with your diet plan. Choose dark chocolate for the bonus of heart-healthy antioxidants.

benefits

Weight-loss diets often fail because they leave you feeling deprived. Integrating favorite foods such as chocolate in controlled portions can help make your weight-loss plan a success. In fact, researchers have found that eating chocolate is associated with greater feelings of well being and happiness, as well as with lower body weight. Dark chocolate is higher than milk chocolate in antioxidants, minerals and plant nutrients that can help protect your heart. For optimal health benefits without overdoing calories, stick with about 1 to 2 ounces per week.

selection and storage

Dark chocolate is available in varying levels of darkness, depending on the percentage of cocoa in it. For example, 60 percent cocoa content means that 40 percent of the product is made of sugar, vanilla and other ingredients. The higher the percentage of cocoa, the less sweet and more bitter it will taste. Dark chocolate includes semisweet and bittersweet varieties. Store dark chocolate, tightly wrapped, in a cool, dry place. Under ideal conditions, it can be stored for years without losing quality.

preparation and serving tips

Dark chocolate is a delicacy that is best enjoyed on its own. It can also be used in baking, in a wide variety of desserts or simply as a garnish for a low-calorie dessert.

nutrients per serving:

Dark Chocolate
1 ounce

Calories 154 **Protein** 1g
Total Fat 9g **Saturated Fat** 5g
Cholesterol 2mg **Carbohydrate** 17g
Dietary Fiber 2g **Sodium** 6mg
Potassium 160mg **Calcium** 16mg
Iron 2.3mg **Magnesium** 43mg
Copper 0.3mg **Phosphorus** 60mg

Dates

Dates are small nuggets of nutrition that satisfy a sweet tooth, making them ideal snacks. Dates are a nutritious substitute for processed sweets like candy.

benefits

Loaded with both soluble and insoluble fiber, dates fill you up and help keep your digestive tract healthy and regular. They are an excellent source of potassium and also provide iron, making them a nutritional powerhouse in a tiny package.

selection and storage

Most supermarkets stock fresh dates in the produce section and dried dates near the raisins. For both types, look for plump fruit with unbroken, smoothly wrinkled skins. Avoid dates that smell bad or have hardened sugar crystals on their skins. Packaged dates are available pitted, unpitted or chopped. Fresh dates should be refrigerated in a tightly sealed container for up to eight months. Stored at room temperature, they'll stay fresh for about a month. Dried dates keep for up to a year in the refrigerator.

preparation and serving tips

Dates are great on their own, but for an extra special treat try stuffing them with whole almonds or chopped walnuts or pecans. For a spicy twist, tuck in a piece of crystallized gingerroot. Add dates to homemade breads, cakes, muffins and cookies for extra richness and nutrition. Dates work well in fruit compotes, salads and desserts. Chopped or slivered, dates can even be sprinkled on side dishes like rice, couscous or vegetables. Chill fresh dates for easier slicing.

nutrients per serving:

Dates, dried
¼ cup

Calories 104
Protein 1g
Total Fat 0g
Saturated Fat 0g
Cholesterol 0mg
Carbohydrate 28g
Dietary Fiber 3g
Sodium 0mg
Potassium 240mg
Calcium 14mg
Iron 0.4mg
Vitamin A 4 IU
Vitamin C 0mg
Folate 7mcg

Edamame

Edamame is the Japanese name for fresh green soybeans. Enjoyed straight from the pod or added to recipes, this tender legume is a satisfying and nutritious way to enjoy soy and all of its health benefits.

benefits

Edamame is low in calories and a rich source of both fiber and protein. These tiny beans are a great substitute for other higher-calorie foods, particularly snack foods, because they fill you up and keep you feeling full for fewer calories. Unlike most plant sources of protein, edamame is a complete protein which means that it contains all of the essential amino acids (building blocks of protein). This makes it a great main ingredient in place of higher-fat meats in vegetarian entrées like stir-fries. It's a good source of iron, potassium and folate, too.

selection and storage

Fresh edamame, in the pods or already shelled, may be available in some supermarkets in the produce section but most often it can be found frozen. Store fresh edamame in the refrigerator for up to two weeks; frozen edamame will last up to six months.

preparation and serving tips

Edamame pods (or shelled soy beans) can be boiled, steamed, sautéed or microwaved. Enjoy edamame directly from the pod alone as a snack or appetizer, or add the beans to a variety of dishes such as stews, salads, soups or pasta for extra fiber and protein. The pod is tough and should be discarded.

nutrients per serving:

Edamame, shelled ½ cup cooked

Calories 95
Protein 8g
Total Fat 4g
Saturated Fat .5g
Cholesterol 0mg
Carbohydrate 8g
Dietary Fiber 4g
Sodium 5mg
Potassium 340mg
Calcium 49mg
Iron 1.7mg
Vitamin A 0 IU
Vitamin C 5mg
Folate 241mcg

bite-you-back roasted edamame

- 2 teaspoons vegetable oil
- 2 teaspoons honey
- ¼ teaspoon wasabi powder*
- 1 package (10 ounces) frozen shelled edamame, thawed
- Kosher salt (optional)

Wasabi powder can be found in the Asian section of most supermarkets and in Asian specialty markets.

1. Preheat oven to 375°F. Combine oil, honey and wasabi powder in large bowl; mix well. Add edamame; toss to coat. Spread on baking sheet in single layer.

2. Bake 12 to 15 minutes or until golden brown, stirring once. Immediately remove to large bowl; sprinkle with salt, if desired. Cool completely before serving. Store in airtight container.

Makes 4 servings

nutrients per serving:

Calories 78
Calories from Fat 46%
Protein 4g
Carbohydrate 7g
Fiber 1g
Total Fat 4g
Saturated Fat 1g
Cholesterol 0mg
Sodium 7mg

Eggplant

Filling and low in calories, this versatile vegetable is part of many popular ethnic dishes, including Indian curries, Greek moussaka, Middle Eastern baba ghanoush and French ratatouille.

benefits

Eggplant's meaty flavor and texture is satisfying and filling, making it popular in vegetarian dishes. Eggplant is also low in calories and a decent source of fiber and potassium. Despite claims that eggplant water, obtained from boiling the raw flesh of eggplant, can aid weight loss by blocking the absorption of fat, there is no research to support this theory.

selection and storage

Choose eggplant that is small, firm and thin-skinned. Larger ones tend to be seedy, tough and bitter. The skin should range in color from deep purple to light violet or white. Eggplant is best used within a few days but may be refrigerated for up to one week.

preparation and serving tips

Eggplant can be eaten with or without the skin; use a potato peeler to easily remove the skin. To help reduce its bitterness, slice the eggplant, season with salt and let it stand for 30 minutes; drain and blot dry before cooking. Eggplant can be baked, roasted, grilled, steamed or sautéed. It is fully cooked when it can be pierced easily with a fork. It tends to absorb fats easily, so go easy on added fats like oil and butter. Eggplant makes a tasty addition to stir-fries, lasagna and pasta dishes. Try stuffing eggplant with flavorful veggies, low-fat cheese and baking for a delightful, decadent dinner.

eggplant and feta stuffed pitas

   2 teaspoons olive oil
   1 cup diced onions
      Nonstick cooking spray
2½ cups diced (unpeeled) eggplant
      (½-inch dice)
   1 medium clove garlic, minced
   1 cup grape tomatoes, quartered
   ¼ cup chopped fresh basil
   3 whole what pitas, warmed and halved
   ¼ cup reduced-fat balsamic vinaigrette
   3 ounces crumbled reduced-fat
      feta cheese

1. Heat oil in large nonstick skillet over medium-high heat. Add onions; spray with cooking spray. Cook and stir 2 minutes. Add eggplant; spray eggplant with cooking spray. Cook and stir 4 to 6 minutes or until eggplant begins to brown. Add garlic; cook and stir 15 seconds. Add tomatoes; cook 2 minutes or until tomatoes are just tender. Remove from heat; stir in basil. Cover; let stand 3 minutes

2. Spoon about ⅓ cup eggplant mixture into each pita half and drizzle with about 1½ teaspoons balsamic vinaigrette. Sprinkle with 1½ tablespoons feta cheese.

Makes 6 servings

nutrients per serving:

Calories 162	**Total Fat** 5g
Calories from Fat 28%	**Saturated Fat** 2g
Protein 7g	**Cholesterol** 4mg
Carbohydrate 25g	**Sodium** 526mg
Fiber 5g	

Egg Whites

On their own, eggs are a moderately lean protein source, but for serious dieters, egg whites are even leaner. Two egg whites or ¼ cup egg substitute have half the calories of a single egg and are fat and cholesterol free.

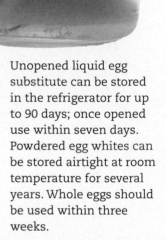

nutrients per serving:

Egg White
1 large

Calories 17
Protein 4g
Total Fat 0g
Saturated Fat 0g
Cholesterol 0mg
Carbohydrate <1g
Dietary Fiber 0g
Sodium 55mg
Potassium 55mg
Calcium 2mg
Iron 0mg
Vitamin A 0 IU
Vitamin C 0mg
Folate 1mcg

benefits

Substituting egg whites or egg substitute for whole eggs is an easy way to cut calories. Egg whites are essentially all protein, which helps to slow digestion and manage your hunger between meals. Liquid egg substitutes are fortified with many of the nutrients lost when the yolk is removed.

selection and storage

You can separate the egg white from the yolk or purchase egg whites as liquids or powders. Liquid products can contain purely egg whites or may contain small amounts of yolk or coloring to give the product a yellow color. Most egg substitutes are pasteurized so you can safely use them in recipes that do not call for cooking.

Unopened liquid egg substitute can be stored in the refrigerator for up to 90 days; once opened use within seven days. Powdered egg whites can be stored airtight at room temperature for several years. Whole eggs should be used within three weeks.

preparation and serving tips

Liquid egg substitute can replace whole eggs in most recipes, both as an ingredient and as the base of an egg dish. Meringue powder (powdered egg whites) is best used in recipes and is perfect for whipping into a meringue. Use egg whites from hard-cooked eggs to make egg salad or add to chopped salads.

nutrients per serving:

Calories 138
Calories from Fat 38%
Protein 13g
Carbohydrate 8g
Fiber 1g
Total Fat 6g
Saturated Fat 3g
Cholesterol 25mg
Sodium 439mg

crustless ham and asparagus quiche

- **2 cups sliced asparagus (½-inch pieces)**
- **1 red bell pepper, cut into ¼-inch dice**
- **1 tablespoon water**
- **1 cup low-fat (1%) milk**
- **2 tablespoons all-purpose flour**
- **4 egg whites**
- **1 whole egg**
- **1 cup chopped cooked deli ham, cut into ¼-inch dice**
- **2 tablespoons chopped fresh tarragon or basil**
- **½ teaspoon salt (optional)**
- **¼ teaspoon black pepper**
- **½ cup (2 ounces) finely shredded Swiss cheese**

1. Preheat oven to 350°F. Combine asparagus, bell pepper and water in large microwavable bowl. Cover and microwave on HIGH 2 minutes or until vegetables are crisp-tender. Drain.

2. Meanwhile, whisk milk and flour in large bowl. Whisk in egg whites and egg until well blended. Stir in vegetables, ham, tarragon, salt, if desired, and black pepper. Pour into 9-inch pie plate.

3. Bake 35 minutes. Sprinkle cheese over quiche; bake 5 minutes or until center is set and cheese is melted. Let stand 5 minutes. *Makes 6 servings*

Variation: Add 1 clove minced garlic and 2 tablespoons chopped green onion.

Fennel

Fennel is often mistaken for celery, but it is much more nutritious and has its own distinctive flavor. An ideal vegetable for dieters, it is low in calories, provides key nutrients and is filling and full of flavor.

benefits

Fennel's unique licorice-like taste enhances other dishes, allowing you to add flavor without also adding calories. Fennel is a good source of potassium and fiber and contains some vitamin C, iron, calcium and folate. Its leaves offer vitamin C and beta-carotene.

nutrients per serving:

Fennel
½ cup raw

Calories 13 **Protein** 1g
Total Fat 0g **Saturated Fat** 0g
Cholesterol 0mg **Carbohydrate** 3g
Dietary Fiber 1g **Sodium** 25mg
Potassium 180mg **Calcium** 21mg
Iron 0.3mg **Vitamin A** 58 IU
Vitamin C 5mg **Folate** 12mcg

selection and storage

Select fennel that has a whitish bulb, white to pale green stalks and light green delicate leaves. The bulb should be firm and free from signs of browning or drying. Store fennel in a plastic bag in the crisper drawer of the refrigerator for up to five days. Fennel seeds are available both ground and whole in the spice section of the supermarket.

preparation and serving tips

All parts of the fennel bulb can be eaten including the stalks, leaves and bulb. Rinse fennel to remove dirt from the bulb and between the stalks. Fennel can be prepared in many ways: braised or sautéed as a side dish, added to soups and stews or even raw in salads. The fragrant greens can be used as a garnish; finely chop and sprinkle on foods just before serving. Try making stuffed fennel bulbs for a vegetarian entrée. Add fennel seed to meatballs or meat loaves for authentic Italian flavor.

nutrients per serving:

Calories 336   **Carbohydrate** 42g   **Saturated Fat** 2g
Calories from Fat 24%   **Fiber** 15g   **Cholesterol** 45mg
Protein 24g   **Total Fat** 9g   **Sodium** 708mg

tuscan-style sausage skillet

2 teaspoons olive oil
½ cup chopped fresh fennel
½ cup chopped sweet or yellow onion
3 cloves garlic, minced
1 can (about 14 ounces) fire-roasted diced tomatoes
1 package (9 ounces) fully cooked chicken or turkey Italian sausage, cut into ½-inch pieces
¾ teaspoon dried rosemary, crushed
1 can (16 ounces) no-salt-added navy or Great Northern beans, drained
4 cups baby spinach or torn spinach

1. Heat oil in large deep skillet over medium-high heat. Add fennel, onion and garlic; cook and stir 5 minutes.

2. Add tomatoes, sausage and rosemary. Reduce heat to low; cover and simmer 10 minutes or until vegetables are tender.

3. Increase heat to medium-high. Stir in beans; cook until heated through.

4. Add spinach. Cover and cook 2 minutes or until spinach is wilted. *Makes 4 servings*

Fish

Fish is a smart catch for dieters. It's low in saturated fat and calories making it the perfect substitute for higher-calorie meats.

nutrients per serving:

Whitefish
3 ounces cooked
Calories 146
Protein 21g
Total Fat 6g
Saturated Fat 1g
Cholesterol 65mg
Carbohydrate 0g
Dietary Fiber 0g
Sodium 55mg
Potassium 345mg
Phosphorus 294mg
Iron 0.4mg
Vitamin B$_{12}$ 0.8mcg
Selenium 14mcg

benefits

The amount of protein in fish is comparable to the amount in meat, making it a wonderful, satisfying alternative. Plus, fish contains omega-3 fatty acids, good unsaturated fats that help prevent heart disease and cancer, treat arthritis, reduce inflammation and depression and improve memory. Some fish like salmon, mackerel, herring, sardines, anchovies and trout are considered fatty because they have more omega-3 fats, which also makes them higher in calories. Leaner fish, including tuna, whitefish, bass, ocean perch and halibut, also provides some omega-3s.

selection and storage

Purchase whole fish, fillets or steaks that are firm and moist. Scales should be shiny and clean, not slimy. If you don't cook fresh fish immediately, store in the refrigerator for one day or wrap well and freeze for up to six months.

preparation and serving tips

To keep fish lean and low in calories, use lower-fat cooking methods and avoid breading and rich sauces. For leaner fish (those with generally lighter color flesh), use moist-heat methods such as poaching or steaming. Dry-heat methods, such as baking, broiling and grilling work well for fatty fish.

Fish cooks fast and is done when it is opaque and the flesh begins to flake. Bake for 8 to 10 minutes per inch of thickness, measured at the thickest point, or grill or broil 4 to 5 minutes per inch of thickness.

skillet fish with lemon tarragon butter

4 teaspoons lemon juice, divided
2 teaspoons reduced-fat margarine
½ teaspoon grated lemon peel
¼ teaspoon prepared mustard
¼ teaspoon dried tarragon leaves
⅛ teaspoon salt
2 lean white fish fillets (4 ounces each),*
    rinsed and patted dry
¼ teaspoon paprika

*Try cod, orange roughy, flounder, haddock, halibut or sole.

1. Whisk 2 teaspoons lemon juice, margarine, lemon peel, mustard, tarragon and salt in small bowl; set aside.

2. Drizzle fillets with remaining 2 teaspoons lemon juice. Sprinkle one side of each fillet with paprika.

3. Spray 12-inch nonstick skillet with nonstick cooking spray; heat over medium heat. Add fish, seasoned side down; cook 3 minutes. Gently turn and cook 3 minutes or until opaque in center and flakes easily when tested with fork. Serve fillets with margarine mixture.

Makes 2 servings

nutrients per serving:

Calories 125
Calories from Fat 24%
Protein 22g
Carbohydrate 1g
Fiber <1g
Total Fat 3g
Saturated Fat 1g
Cholesterol 60mg
Sodium 291mg

Flax Seed

Flax seed may be tiny, but it's quite impressive when it comes to helping with weight loss. To unlock its potential, flax seed must be ground before eating.

benefits

Its high fiber content—a whopping 2 grams in just 1 tablespoon—and healthy fat make flax seed a fabulous food for weight loss and weight maintenance. In fact, many dieters have found that adding flax seed to their diet helps them manage hunger because it keeps them feeling satisfied for longer. Add flax seed to your diet gradually to let your body adjust to the increased fiber, and be sure to drink plenty of water.

selection and storage

Flax seed is available whole or already ground into meal. Because ground flax will go rancid more quickly, it's better to buy whole flax seed and grind it yourself (this takes just seconds in a food processor or blender). Once ground, flax seed should be stored in an airtight container in the freezer and used within a few weeks. Whole flax seed stays fresh up to one year if stored in a cool, dark, dry place.

preparation and serving tips

Flax seed has a pleasant nutty flavor, but is almost undetectable when added to many foods. A few tablespoons of ground flax seed can be added to baked goods, such as breads, muffins, cookies and pancakes. Sprinkle over cottage cheese, yogurt, cereal, salads or add it to smoothies. It can be cooked into meat loaves, meatballs and casseroles as well. Flax can also be used as an egg substitute in baked goods. To replace one egg, grind 1 tablespoon of flax seed in a food processor. Add 3 tablespoons of water and process until smooth.

nutrients per serving:

Flax Seed
1 tablespoon ground

Calories 37 **Protein** 1g **Total Fat** 3g **Saturated Fat** 0g **Cholesterol** 0mg **Carbohydrate** 2g **Dietary Fiber** 2g **Sodium** 0mg **Potassium** 60mg **Calcium** 18mg **Iron** 0.4mg **Phosphorus** 45mg **Magnesium** 27mg

Grapefruit

Despite its reputation as a "fat-burner," grapefruit has no special ability to melt away excess fat. What makes it an important part of any diet is that it offers a lot of nutrition for very few calories.

benefits

Grapefruit's virtues—low in calories and full of soluble fiber—will help you lose weight, just not as miraculously as rumor has it. Its soluble fiber content will help fill you up and prevent overeating. Grapefruit is also an excellent source of vitamin C, and the pink and red varieties are good sources of disease-fighting beta-carotene. For an additional helping of soluble fiber, peel a grapefruit and eat the membranes like you do an orange.

selection and storage

Grapefruit is only available when fully ripe. Choose grapefruit that feels heavy, as it will be juicier. Avoid those that are soft or mushy, or oblong rather than round. The difference in taste among white, red and pink varieties of grapefruit is minimal; they are equally sweet and tart. Store grapefruit in the crisper drawer of the refrigerator for up to two months.

preparation and serving tips

Wash grapefruit before cutting to prevent bacteria on the skin from touching the flesh. Bring it to room temperature before you juice or slice it for greater flavor. Beyond the typical halved grapefruit at breakfast, try peeling and eating it like an orange for a juicy, mouthwatering snack or enjoy it on top of a salad with some healthy nuts. For dessert, sprinkle with a little brown sugar and place it under the broiler until it bubbles.

nutrients per serving:

**Grapefruit
½ medium**

Calories 41
Protein 1g
Total Fat 0g
Saturated Fat 0g
Cholesterol 0mg
Carbohydrate 10g
Dietary Fiber 1.5g
Sodium 0mg
Potassium 180mg
Calcium 15mg
Iron 0.1mg
Vitamin A 1,187 IU
Vitamin C 44mg
Folate 13mcg

Grapes

Grapes are portable and convenient and eating them offers the same soothing hand-to-mouth action that other sweet snacks provide, but with fewer calories.

benefits

Grapes are a refreshing low-calorie substitute for high-fat, calorie-filled snacks and desserts and are perfect for dieters craving something sweet. High in water and a respectable source of fiber, grapes are filling and provide only about 60 calories per 1-cup serving. Grapes also contain a collection of powerful phytonutrients that may help fight cancer and heart disease.

selection and storage

When buying grapes, look for clusters with plump, well-colored fruit attached to pliable, green stems. Soft or wrinkled grapes or those with browned areas around the stem are past their prime. Whether green, red or blue/black, good color is the key to flavor. The sweetest green grapes are yellow-green in color, red varieties that are predominantly crimson/red will have the best flavor and blue/purple varieties taste best if their color is deep and rich, almost black. Most are available seedless. Stored unwashed in the refrigerator, they'll keep up to a week.

preparation and serving tips

Rinse grape clusters just before eating. Chilling enhances the flavor and texture of grapes; cold sliced grapes taste great blended in with low-fat yogurt and frozen grapes make a popular summer treat. For a change of pace, skewer grapes, banana slices, apple chunks and pineapple cubes and brush with a combination of honey, lemon juice and ground nutmeg and broil until warm.

nutrients per serving:

Grapes
½ cup

Calories 31 **Protein** 0g **Total Fat** 0g
Saturated Fat 0g **Cholesterol** 0mg
Carbohydrate 8g **Dietary Fiber** <1g
Sodium 0mg **Potassium** 90mg
Calcium 6mg **Iron** 0.1mg
Vitamin A 46 IU **Vitamin C** 2mg
Folate 2mcg

nutty fruit kabobs

- 1 large apple, cut into 24 pieces
- 1 tablespoon lemon juice
- 1 can (8 ounces) pineapple chunks in juice
- 24 miniature marshmallows
- 1 cup seedless green or red grapes
- ½ cup plain yogurt
- ½ cup creamy peanut butter

1. Combine apple and lemon juice in large bowl; toss to coat. Drain pineapple, reserving 4 teaspoons juice.

2. Thread apple pieces, marshmallows, grapes and pineapple onto small skewers.

3. Whisk yogurt and peanut butter in medium bowl until smooth. Stir in reserved 4 teaspoons pineapple juice. Serve fruit skewers with peanut butter sauce for dipping.

Makes 6 servings

Tips: Six-inch wooden skewers can be used for this recipe. Or omit skewers and spoon fruit and marshmallows into six small serving dishes and drizzle with peanut butter sauce.

nutrients per serving:

Calories 210
Calories from Fat 48%
Protein 7g
Carbohydrate 24g
Fiber 3g
Total Fat 11g
Saturated Fat 2.5g
Cholesterol 0mg
Sodium 115mg

Greek Yogurt

If you're looking for a new light snack or breakfast to fill you up while you slim down, you'll appreciate Greek yogurt. This Mediterranean-style yogurt is creamier and thicker than regular yogurt and contains almost double the protein and fewer carbohydrates.

benefits

Rich in lean protein, Greek yogurt can help provide long-lasting energy, which helps stretch out the duration between meals and snacks. The triple-straining process used to remove whey (liquid) is what makes Greek yogurt so creamy. That process also lowers the lactose content, making it easier for some people to digest. If you're watching salt intake, Greek yogurt is a better choice than regular yogurt—it has almost 50 percent less sodium. It's also a good source of calcium and potassium, important nutrients that you may be lacking as you cut calories. Like its regular yogurt relations, Greek yogurt contains healthful bacteria, or probiotics, to help keep your immune system and digestive tract healthy.

selection and storage

Greek yogurt is a newcomer to the yogurt aisle, but its growing popularity is bringing it to most supermarkets. Like regular yogurt, it is available in nonfat, low-fat and whole-milk varieties; flavors vary from plain to vanilla to fruit-filled. You'll also find a Mediterranean-influenced honey flavor. Like all yogurt, Greek yogurt should be stored in the refrigerator and used within about two weeks.

preparation and serving tips

Greek yogurt can be enjoyed straight from the carton or used as a base to make healthy salad dressings, dips, sauces, smoothies, yogurt-based ice creams and desserts. Also try using plain Greek yogurt as a substitute for sour cream.

nutrients per serving:

Greek Yogurt, nonfat ½ cup

Calories 80
Protein 11g
Total Fat 0g
Saturated Fat 0g
Cholesterol 0mg
Carbohydrate 9g
Dietary Fiber 0g
Sodium 45mg
Potassium 160mg
Calcium 150mg
Iron 0mg
Vitamin A 0 IU
Vitamin C 0mg
Folate 0mcg

chicken salad pitas with yogurt sauce

1½ cups diced cooked chicken breast
½ cup red seedless grapes, halved if large
1 stalk celery, trimmed and chopped
2½ tablespoons plain nonfat Greek yogurt
2 tablespoons fat-free mayonnaise
¼ teaspoon salt
⅛ teaspoon black pepper
⅛ teaspoon chili powder
⅛ teaspoon curry powder
2 whole wheat pitas, cut in half
4 lettuce leaves
1 tablespoon sliced almonds

nutrients per serving:

Calories 178
Calories from Fat 15%
Protein 20g
Carbohydrate 20g
Fiber 3g
Total Fat 3g
Saturated Fat 1g
Cholesterol 41mg
Sodium 410mg

1. Combine chicken, grapes and celery in medium bowl. Whisk yogurt, mayonnaise, salt, pepper, chili powder and curry powder in small bowl. Add to chicken mixture; mix well.

2. Line pita halves with lettuce. Spoon chicken mixture into each pita half and sprinkle with sliced almonds. Serve immediately.

Makes 4 servings

Green Beans

Easy to prepare and a pleasure to eat, green beans (also known as snap beans) are a favorite vegetable for many. Their low-calorie profile and versatility make green beans a great vegetable choice for dieters.

benefits

Green beans help to fill you up, not out—important when you're trying to lose weight. The large volume per serving makes it easy to get your recommended 2 to 3 cups of vegetables per day. Besides being low in calories and a decent source of fiber, green beans are also rich in carotenoids, including lutein for healthy vision and beta-carotene for reduced cancer risk.

selection and storage

Fresh green beans are at their peak from May to October. Choose slender beans that are crisp, brightly colored and without blemishes. Store in the refrigerator in a plastic bag for up to five days. Frozen green beans are available and come very close nutritionally. Canned green beans are also an option, but they may lose some vitamins in processing and typically contain more sodium.

preparation and serving tips

Fresh or frozen green beans can be steamed lightly on the stove or in the microwave until just crisp-tender. Canned green beans should be rinsed to lower the sodium and heated gently to prevent them from getting mushy. Green beans stand up well as a side dish, lightly seasoned with herbs or sprinkled with toasted nuts. They also work well in soups and casseroles. Raw green beans make a great snack with a low-fat dip and add lots of crunch and volume to salads.

nutrients per serving:

Green Beans
½ cup cooked

Calories 22 **Protein** 1g **Total Fat** 0g **Saturated Fat** 0g
Cholesterol 0mg **Carbohydrate** 5g **Dietary Fiber** 2g
Sodium 0mg **Potassium** 90mg **Calcium** 28mg **Iron** 0.4mg
Vitamin A 438 IU **Vitamin C** 6mg **Folate** 21mcg

green bean rice with almonds

   2 tablespoons reduced-fat margarine
   ½ cup finely chopped onion
   1¼ cups fat-free reduced-sodium
        chicken or vegetable broth
   ½ teaspoon lemon pepper seasoning
   1 cup diagonally sliced green beans
   1¼ cups uncooked instant white rice
   3 tablespoons sliced almonds, toasted*

To toast almonds, place in small dry skillet. Cook over medium heat 1 to 2 minutes until almonds are lightly browned, stirring constantly.

1. Melt margarine in medium saucepan over medium heat. Add onion; cook and stir 5 minutes or until onion is tender. Add broth and lemon pepper seasoning; bring to a boil over high heat. Add green beans; reduce heat to low. Cover and simmer 7 minutes or until green beans are tender, stirring occasionally.

2. Stir in rice; cover and remove from heat. Let stand 5 minutes or until liquid is absorbed and rice is tender. Fluff with fork; stir in almonds. Serve immediately.

Makes 6 servings

nutrients per serving:

Calories 128
Calories from Fat 28%
Protein 3g
Carbohydrate 20g
Fiber 1g

Total Fat 4g
Saturated Fat 1g
Cholesterol 0mg
Sodium 53mg

Green Peas

Like other legumes, peas are a dieter's friend—high in nutrients yet low in calories. Green peas are also known as English or garden peas, and can be enjoyed raw or cooked after they are removed from their pods.

benefits

Green peas have the ideal nutrient profile for weight-loss diets—low in calories, yet rich in fiber, protein and key vitamins and minerals. They contain twice the protein of most vegetables and are also a good source of pectin and other soluble fiber that can help lower cholesterol and leave you feeling full and satisfied. Of the several nutrients peas provide, iron is particularly noteworthy as it's hard to find plant sources of this blood-building mineral.

selection and storage

Fresh peas are available during the spring and fall. Choose firm, plump, bright green pods. Store fresh peas in the refrigerator and eat within a few days; their sugar quickly turns to starch so the sooner you eat them the more flavorful they'll be. Canned and frozen peas are also convenient and nutritious. Just be sure to rinse canned peas to lower the sodium.

preparation and serving tips

Wash fresh peas just before shelling. Steam fresh or frozen green peas 6 to 8 minutes or just until heated through to retain flavor and vitamin C. Cook canned peas just until warm to prevent them from getting mushy. Peas are versatile and can be added to salads, soups, casseroles, pasta sauce or simply enjoyed as a side dish alone or mixed with other vegetables.

nutrients per serving:

Green Peas
½ cup cooked

Calories 67
Protein 4g
Total Fat 0g
Saturated Fat 0g
Cholesterol 0mg
Carbohydrate 13g
Dietary Fiber 4.5g
Sodium 0mg
Potassium 220mg
Calcium 22mg
Iron 1.2mg
Vitamin A 641 IU
Vitamin C 11mg
Folate 50mcg

main-dish chicken soup

6 cups fat-free reduced-sodium
   chicken broth
1 cup grated carrots
½ cup diced red bell pepper
½ cup frozen green peas
½ cup sliced green onions
1 seedless cucumber
12 chicken tenders (about 1 pound),
   halved
½ teaspoon white pepper

1. Bring broth to a boil in Dutch oven. Add carrots, bell pepper, peas and green onions. Return to a boil. Reduce heat to low; simmer 3 minutes.

2. Meanwhile, cut ends off cucumber and discard. Using vegetable peeler, start at top and make long, noodle-like strips of cucumber. Cut any remaining cucumber pieces into thin slices. Add cucumber to Dutch oven; cook 2 minutes.

3. Add chicken tenders and white pepper; simmer 5 minutes or until chicken is cooked through.   *Makes 6 servings*

nutrients per serving:

Calories 158
Calories from Fat 15%
Protein 26g
Carbohydrate 7g
Fiber 2g
Total Fat 3g
Saturated Fat <1g
Cholesterol 68mg
Sodium 304mg

Green Tea

For a refreshing and satisfying low-calorie way to rev up your metabolism, try adding freshly brewed green tea to your diet.

benefits

Research has found that people who drink caffeinated green tea lose more weight than those who don't. The findings have not yet been attributed to any particular green tea property but may simply be the result of the impact of caffeine on metabolism, increasing it and making the body burn more calories and fat. It's also possible that drinking zero-calorie liquids like tea may delay hunger and prevent overeating as they provide a sense of fullness. The verdict is still out on whether or not the high levels of antioxidants in green tea help lower blood cholesterol and blood pressure.

selection and storage

There are many different varieties of green tea available, both loose or in tea bags. Be aware that prepared iced green tea may contain added sugar. Store tea in an airtight container in a cool, dry place.

preparation and serving tips

Green tea is best brewed at a lower temperature (140°F to 180°F) to prevent a bitter taste. Steep tea for 30 seconds to 2 minutes, depending on your taste preference. To retain antioxidants when making iced tea, pour strong hot tea over ice.

nutrients per serving:

Green Tea
1 cup brewed

Calories 4
Protein <1g
Total Fat 0g
Saturated Fat 0g
Cholesterol 0mg
Carbohydrate <1g
Dietary Fiber <1g
Sodium 5mg
Potassium 30mg
Calcium 6mg
Vitamin A 0 IU
Vitamin C 12mg
Folate 32mcg

mint-green tea coolers

2 green tea bags
4 thin slices fresh ginger
  (about 1 inch long)
7 or 8 large fresh mint leaves,
  roughly torn
2 cups boiling water
  Crushed ice

1. Place tea bags, ginger and mint leaves in teapot or 2-cup heatproof measuring cup. Add boiling water; steep 4 minutes. Remove and discard tea bags, ginger and mint leaves.

2. Cool tea to room temperature. Serve over crushed ice.

Makes 2 servings

Tip: For extra flavor, squeeze a lime wedge into each cooler before serving.

Jicama

Often referred to as a Mexican potato, this easily overlooked root vegetable is refreshingly crisp and crunchy with a sweet, nutty flavor and radishlike texture.

benefits

Fibrous foods like jicama that have a high water content and ample fiber help fill you up and control your appetite. They also take longer to chew, giving your brain time to get the signal that you've had enough to eat. Jicama is very low in calories, almost sodium free and an excellent source of vitamin C.

selection and storage

Jicama is available in most supermarkets from November through May. Select jicama that are firm and unblemished with a slightly silky sheen. They should not feel soft or have bruises or wrinkles, which signal that they've been stored for too long. Jicama can be stored for up to two weeks in a plastic bag in the refrigerator. You may also find jicama presliced and packaged.

preparation and serving tips

Jicama is a versatile vegetable that adds a crisp and nutty sweetness to your favorite recipes. The thin skin of a jicama should be peeled before eating or cooking. Cut jicama into cubes or sticks and add it to salads, salsa or coleslaw or simply enjoy it as a snack. It can also be added to stir-fries or roasted with other vegetables. For a refreshing salad, combine cubed jicama, sliced cucumber and orange sections; sprinkle with chili powder and salt and drizzle with lemon juice.

nutrients per serving:

Jicama
½ cup raw

Calories 25 **Protein** <1g **Total Fat** 0g **Saturated Fat** 0g
Cholesterol 0mg **Carbohydrate** 6g **Dietary Fiber** 3g
Sodium 5mg **Potassium** 100mg **Calcium** 8mg **Iron** 0.4mg
Vitamin A 14 IU **Vitamin C** 13mg **Folate** 8mcg

jerk turkey salad

   6 ounces boneless turkey breast tenderloin
1½ teaspoons Caribbean jerk seasoning
   4 cups mixed salad greens
   ¾ cup sliced peeled cucumber
   ⅔ cup chopped fresh pineapple
   ⅔ cup raspberries or quartered strawberries
   ½ cup slivered peeled jicama or sliced celery
   1 green onion, sliced
   ¼ cup lime juice
   3 tablespoons honey

1. Prepare grill for direct cooking. Rub turkey with jerk seasoning. Grill turkey over medium heat 15 to 20 minutes or until turkey is cooked through, turning once. Remove from grill; let stand until cool enough to handle.

2. Cut turkey into bite-size pieces. Combine turkey, greens, cucumber, pineapple, raspberries, jicama and green onion in large bowl.

3. Combine lime juice and honey. Pour over salad; toss to coat. Serve immediately.

Makes 2 servings

nutrients per serving:

Calories 265
Calories from Fat 6%
Protein 17g
Carbohydrate 48g
Fiber 6g
Total Fat 2g
Saturated Fat 1g
Cholesterol 34mg
Sodium 356mg

Leeks

Their onionlike appearance is no coincidence; leeks are a slightly sweeter and less intense relative of onions and garlic.

benefits

Because leeks are so flavorful, you can add them to many dishes and skip the high-fat sauces and butter. At less than 20 calories per serving, leeks are a caloric bargain. Phytonutrients in leeks, like those in onions and garlic, are associated with a decreased risk of cancer. They may also help lower blood pressure and prevent clotting, both of which reduce the risk of heart disease.

selection and storage

Leeks are available year-round. Choose leeks with crisp, bright green leaves and an unblemished white portion. Smaller leeks will be more tender. Store leeks in a plastic bag in the refrigerator for up to five days.

preparation and serving tips

Slit the leeks from top to bottom and wash thoroughly to remove the dirt trapped between leaf layers. Although the entire leek is edible, most people prefer to eat the white fleshy base and tender inner leaves and discard the bitter dark green leaves. Try using leeks in place of onions for a sweeter, mellow flavor in soups or vegetable dishes. You can also add them to salads and salad dressings for extra flavor. Sautéed in a little olive oil, they make a tasty and healthy side dish. Try grilling them whole and serving them sliced at your next summer barbecue.

nutrients per serving:

Leeks
½ cup cooked

Calories 16
Protein <1g
Total Fat 0g
Saturated Fat 0g
Cholesterol 0mg
Carbohydrate 4g
Dietary Fiber 0.5g
Sodium 5mg
Potassium 45mg
Calcium 16mg
Iron 0.6mg
Vitamin A 422 IU
Vitamin C 2mg
Folate 12mcg

polenta lasagna

4¼ cups water, divided

1½ cups whole grain yellow cornmeal

4 teaspoons finely chopped fresh
    marjoram

1 teaspoon olive oil

1 pound fresh mushrooms, sliced

1 cup chopped leeks

1 clove garlic, minced

½ cup (2 ounces) shredded part-skim
    mozzarella cheese

2 tablespoons chopped fresh basil

1 tablespoon chopped fresh oregano

⅛ teaspoon black pepper

2 medium red bell peppers, chopped

¼ cup freshly grated Parmesan
    cheese, divided

1. Bring 4 cups water to a boil in medium saucepan over high heat. Slowly whisk in cornmeal. Reduce heat to low; stir in marjoram. Simmer 15 to 20 minutes or until polenta thickens and pulls away from side of saucepan. Spread in ungreased 13×9-inch baking pan. Cover and refrigerate about 1 hour or until firm.

2. Preheat oven to 350°F. Spray 11×7-inch baking dish with nonstick cooking spray. Heat oil in medium nonstick skillet over medium heat. Add mushrooms, leeks and garlic; cook and stir 5 minutes or until leeks are crisp-tender. Stir in mozzarella cheese, basil, oregano and black pepper.

3. Place bell peppers and remaining ¼ cup water in food processor or blender; process until smooth.

4. Cut polenta into twelve 3½-inch squares; arrange six squares in bottom of prepared dish. Spread with half of bell pepper mixture, half of vegetable mixture and 2 tablespoons Parmesan cheese. Repeat layers. Bake 20 minutes or until cheese is melted and polenta is golden.   *Makes 6 servings*

nutrients per serving:

Calories 195

Calories from Fat 21%

Protein 9g

Carbohydrate 31g

Fiber 4g

Total Fat 5g

Saturated Fat 2g

Cholesterol 9mg

Sodium 128mg

Lemons

With tart juice and a zesty peel, lemons can add life to everything from fish to vegetables to tea and perk up the fresh, low-calorie foods in your weight-loss plan.

nutrients per serving:

Lemon juice of 1 medium

Calories 12
Protein <1g
Total Fat 0g
Saturated Fat 0g
Cholesterol 0mg
Carbohydrate 4g
Dietary Fiber 0.2g
Sodium 0mg
Potassium 58mg
Calcium 3mg
Iron 0mg
Vitamin A 9 IU
Vitamin C 22mg
Folate 6mcg

benefits

When it comes to watching your waistline, lemon juice added to water can help suppress a ravenous appetite. Added to hot beverages, it can be a natural treatment for constipation. Lemons have been studied for potential positive effects on metabolism, although the evidence to support this is lacking. They are packed with vitamin C, the antioxidant that helps fight heart disease, inflammation and cancer, and the peel is rich in an antioxidant called rutin that may play a role in strengthening the walls of blood vessels.

selection and storage

Lemon varieties vary mostly in their skin thickness, juiciness and number of seeds. Look for firm, unblemished lemons that are heavy for their size (this indicates juiciness). Thin-skinned fruit yields the most juice. Refrigerated, they keep for a month or two.

preparation and serving tips

To get more juice from a lemon, bring it to room temperature and firmly roll it back and forth on the countertop before slicing and juicing. Grated lemon peel makes a great addition to desserts, fruit salads and salad dressings. Be sure to wash lemons thoroughly, then grate the peel with a fine grater or citrus zester. Avoid the bitter white pith.

seafood tacos with fruit salsa

Fruit Salsa (recipe follows)
2 tablespoons lemon juice
1 teaspoon chili powder
1 teaspoon ground allspice
1 teaspoon grated lemon peel
1 teaspoon olive oil
1 teaspoon minced garlic
½ teaspoon ground cloves
1 pound halibut or snapper fillets
12 (6-inch) corn tortillas or 6 (7- to 8-inch) flour tortillas
3 cups shredded romaine lettuce
1 small red onion, halved and thinly sliced

1. Prepare Fruit Salsa. Adjust grid 4 to 6 inches above heat; spray with nonstick cooking spray. Preheat grill to medium-high heat.

2. Combine lemon juice, chili powder, allspice, lemon peel, oil, garlic and cloves in small bowl. Rub fish with spice mixture.

3. Grill fish, covered, 3 minutes or until lightly browned on bottom. Carefully turn over; grill 2 minutes or until opaque in center. Remove from heat and cut into pieces, removing bones if necessary.

4. Place tortillas on grill in single layer. Heat 5 to 10 seconds; turn and cook 5 to 10 seconds or until heated through.

5. Top each tortilla with lettuce, red onion, fish and 2 tablespoons Fruit Salsa.

Makes 6 servings

fruit salsa

1 small ripe papaya, peeled, seeded and diced
1 firm small banana, diced
2 green onions, minced
2 jalapeño peppers, seeded and minced
3 tablespoons chopped fresh cilantro
3 tablespoons lime juice

Combine all ingredients in medium bowl.

Makes ¾ cup

nutrients per serving:

Calories 294	**Fiber** 6g
Calories from Fat 14%	**Total Fat** 5g
Protein 21g	**Saturated Fat** 1g
Carbohydrate 43g	**Cholesterol** 24mg
	Sodium 296mg

Lentils

Lentils are a great source of low-fat protein and make a perfect low-calorie substitute for higher-calorie meats while also supplying a generous amount of nutrients.

benefits

Lentils are high in fiber and protein, making them perfect for dieters. Fiber provides bulk that promotes the feeling of fullness and also helps lower blood cholesterol. The protein offers long-lasting satisfaction to fight hunger. Lentils are exceptionally high in folate, which may help prevent heart disease and dementia. Lentils are an important source of iron for vegetarians, protecting against anemia.

selection and storage

Brown, green and red lentils are the most common varieties in the United States. If you buy them packaged, look for well-sealed bags with brightly colored and uniformly sized lentils. If you buy them in bulk, watch for holes, which indicates insect infestation. Store lentils in an airtight container at a cool temperature for up to a year.

preparation and serving tips

Red lentils cook quickly and become mushy, so they work best in soups, purées or dips. Brown and green lentils retain their shape if not overcooked and can be used in salads or any dish in which you want firmer lentils. Most lentils cook in 30 to 45 minutes or less and don't require any precooking or soaking like dried beans do. Although great on their own, lentils can also easily be flavored with herbs and spices.

nutrients per serving:

Lentils
½ cup cooked

Calories 115 *Protein* 9g *Total Fat* 0g *Saturated Fat* 0g
Cholesterol 0mg *Carbohydrate* 20g *Dietary Fiber* 8g
Sodium 0mg *Potassium* 365mg *Calcium* 19mg
Iron 3.3mg *Vitamin A* 8 IU *Vitamin C* 2mg *Folate* 179mcg

lentil burgers

- 1 can (about 14½ ounces) fat-free reduced-sodium chicken or vegetable broth
- 1 cup dried lentils, sorted and rinsed
- 1 small carrot, grated
- ¼ cup coarsely chopped mushrooms
- 1 egg
- ¼ cup plain dry bread crumbs
- 3 tablespoons finely chopped onion
- 2 cloves garlic, minced
- 1 teaspoon dried thyme
- ¼ cup plain nonfat yogurt
- ¼ cup chopped seeded cucumber
- ½ teaspoon dried mint
- ¼ teaspoon dried dill weed
- ¼ teaspoon black pepper
- ⅛ teaspoon salt
  Hamburger buns (optional)

1. Bring broth to a boil in medium saucepan over high heat. Stir in lentils; reduce heat to low. Cover and simmer about 30 minutes or until lentils are tender and liquid is absorbed. Cool to room temperature.

2. Place lentils, carrot and mushrooms in food processor or blender; process until finely chopped but not smooth. (Some whole lentils should still be visible.) Stir in egg, bread crumbs, onion, garlic and thyme. Cover and refrigerate 2 to 3 hours.

3. Combine yogurt, cucumber, mint, dill, black pepper and salt in small bowl. Set aside.

4. Shape lentil mixture into four ½-inch-thick patties. Spray large skillet with cooking spray; heat over medium-low heat. Cook patties about 5 minutes per side or until browned. Serve yogurt sauce over burgers on hamburger buns, if desired.
Makes 4 servings

nutrients per serving:

Calories 124	**Total Fat** 2g
Calories from Fat 14%	**Saturated Fat** 1g
Protein 9g	**Cholesterol** 54mg
Carbohydrate 21g	**Sodium** 166mg
Fiber 1g	

Lettuce

Dieters have long loved lettuce for good reason; variations in color, texture and flavor provide crunchy leafy goodness for very few calories.

nutrients per serving:

**Lettuce, romaine
1 cup**

Calories 8
Protein 1g
Total Fat 0g
Saturated Fat 0g
Cholesterol 0mg
Carbohydrate 2g
Dietary Fiber 1g
Sodium 5mg
Potassium 115mg
Calcium 16mg
Iron 0.5mg
Vitamin A 4,094 IU
Vitamin C 11mg
Folate 64mcg

benefits

Eat a lettuce salad before a meal to take the edge off your hunger and curb your appetite, making it less likely you'll overindulge. Lettuce takes time to chew, giving your stomach a chance to signal to the brain that it's getting full. Dark green lettuces such as romaine, endive, escarole, looseleaf, butterhead, arugula and watercress are the most nutritious. Generally, the darker the color, the more nutrients it has.

selection and storage

There are hundreds of varieties of lettuce, many available in your regular supermarket. Choose lettuce that is crisp and free of blemishes. When choosing a bag of prewashed salad greens, look for crisp, bright leaves with no discoloration. Store all lettuce in an airtight bag or container in the refrigerator for three to five days.

preparation and storage

For heads of lettuce, remove the leaves, wash and drain completely or blot with a paper towel to remove excess moisture. Combine lettuce with fresh fruits or vegetables, cold pasta or chunks of chicken or tuna to make a nutritious low-calorie main dish; just go easy on the salad dressing and high-calorie toppings. For an appetite-suppressing meal starter, make a salad with a variety of deep green lettuces dressed with a little flavored vinegar, lemon juice and oil.

new wave chicken salad wraps

2 cups chopped fresh spinach
1½ cups chopped cooked chicken breast
   (about 8 ounces uncoooked)
1 cup chopped fresh tomatoes
1 cup shredded carrots
1 cup frozen corn, thawed
¼ cup reduced-fat mayonnaise
2 teaspoons garlic-herb seasoning
16 leaves romaine, iceberg or bibb lettuce

1. Combine all ingredients except lettuce in large bowl; mix well.

2. Spoon ¼ cup chicken mixture onto each lettuce leaf. Serve immediately.

Makes 8 servings (2 wraps each)

nutrients per serving:

Calories 93
Calories from Fat 31%
Protein 9g
Carbohydrate 7g
Fiber 2g
Total Fat 3g
Saturated Fat <1g
Cholesterol 23mg
Sodium 98mg

Limes

A squeeze of lime juice and a pinch of freshly grated peel can perk up almost any low-calorie dish.

benefits

Lime juice is a great flavor enhancer, helping to make low-calorie meals more enjoyable. Added to water, lime juice can increase the amount you drink, filling your stomach and reducing the amount you eat. Limes provide a hefty amount of vitamin C, which helps boost immunity. They also contain powerful phytonutrients that help prevent heart disease and cancer.

selection and storage

The most common variety is the Persian lime. The key lime, best known for its role in key lime pie, is small and round, while the Persian lime looks like a small green lemon. Limes typically turn yellowish as they ripen. The greenest limes have the best flavor, and key limes are generally more flavorful because of their greater acidity. Refrigerated, limes keep for a month or two. Unsweetened bottled lime juice is available as well.

preparation and serving tips

Lime juice can be used to add tang to meat and fish dishes, and a splash of lime juice over fruit salad prevents discoloration. To get more juice from a lime, bring it to room temperature and firmly roll it back and forth on the countertop before cutting and juicing. Add grated lime peel to salads, dressings and desserts for a potent lime flavor.

nutrients per serving:

Lime
juice of 1 medium

Calories 20 **Protein** <1g **Total Fat** 0g **Saturated Fat** 0g
Cholesterol 0mg **Carbohydrate** 7g **Dietary Fiber** 2g
Sodium 0mg **Potassium** 70mg **Calcium** 22mg **Iron** 0.4mg
Vitamin A 34 IU **Vitamin C** 20mg **Folate** 5mcg

thai grilled chicken

- **4 boneless skinless chicken breasts** (about 1¼ pounds)
- **¼ cup low-sodium soy sauce**
- **2 teaspoons minced garlic**
- **½ teaspoon red pepper flakes**
- **2 tablespoons honey**
- **1 tablespoon fresh lime juice**

1. Prepare grill for direct cooking. Place chicken in shallow baking dish. Combine soy sauce, garlic and red pepper flakes in small bowl. Pour over chicken, turning to coat. Let stand 10 minutes.

2. Meanwhile, whisk honey and lime juice in small bowl.

3. Place chicken on grid over medium heat; brush with soy sauce marinade. Discard remaining marinade. Grill, covered, 5 minutes. Brush both sides of chicken with honey mixture. Grill other side 5 minutes or until chicken is cooked through.

Makes 4 servings

nutrients per serving:

Calories 140
Calories from Fat 7%
Protein 22g
Carbohydrate 10g
Fiber <1g
Total Fat 1g
Saturated Fat <1g
Cholesterol 53mg
Sodium 349mg

Milk

nutrients per serving:

Milk, fat-free (skim) 1 cup

Calories 83
Protein 8g
Total Fat 0g
Saturated Fat 0g
Cholesterol 5mg
Carbohydrate 12g
Dietary Fiber 0g
Sodium 105mg
Potassium 380mg
Calcium 299mg
Iron 0.1mg
Vitamin A 37 IU
Vitamin C 0mg
Folate 12mcg

benefits

Emerging research connects key milk nutrients, particularly calcium and vitamin D, with weight loss, although the reason for this connection is not known. It may simply be that milk drinkers replace soda and other high-calorie beverages with protein-rich milk. Milk also delivers nine essential nutrients that are often lacking when you cut back on calories.

selection and storage

Milk varies in the percentage of fat: whole (4%), reduced-fat (2%), low-fat (1%) and fat-free (skim). While there is a significant difference in fat and calories between whole and fat-free milk, there is no difference in other nutrients. All milk containers should have a "sell-by" date and will stay fresh about seven days after this date. Avoid raw, or unpasteurized, milk as it may carry bacteria that can make you sick. Powdered milk is also available.

preparation and serving tips

Milk tastes best when served very cold. Most recipes work fine with lower-fat milk varieties, making it easy to cut calories and fat. Try using nonfat evaporated milk in recipes that call for whole milk or cream, such as for sauces and cream soups. Powdered milk makes a great addition to blender drinks, soups and casseroles.

old-fashioned macaroni & cheese with broccoli

- **2 cups (8 ounces) uncooked elbow macaroni**
- **3 cups small broccoli florets**
- **1 tablespoon reduced-fat margarine**
- **1 tablespoon all-purpose flour**
- **½ teaspoon salt**
- **⅛ teaspoon black pepper**
- **1¾ cups fat-free (skim) milk**
- **1½ cups (6 ounces) shredded reduced-fat sharp Cheddar cheese**

1. Cook pasta according to package directions. Add broccoli during last 5 minutes of cooking. Drain pasta and broccoli; return to pan.

2. Meanwhile, melt margarine in small saucepan over medium heat. Whisk in flour, salt and pepper; cook and stir 1 minute. Stir in milk; bring to a boil over medium-high heat, stirring frequently. Reduce heat and simmer 2 minutes. Remove from heat. Gradually stir in cheese until melted. Stir sauce into pasta and broccoli. *Makes 8 servings*

nutrients per serving:

Calories 205
Calories from Fat 26%
Protein 12g
Carbohydrate 28g
Fiber 2g
Total Fat 6g
Saturated Fat 3g
Cholesterol 16mg
Sodium 371mg

Mushrooms

The meaty texture of mushrooms makes them a perfect substitute for meat, as any vegetarian can tell you. Plus, mushrooms are the only source of vitamin D in the produce aisle.

benefits

Besides being very low in calories and a decent source of fiber, mushrooms are virtually fat free and very low in sodium. When building your plate to maximize vitamin D, consider mushrooms; they're the only plant source of vitamin D and one of the few nonfortified food sources. They produce vitamin D following exposure to sunlight, which is essential for bone health and is being studied for its role in weight loss, as well as the prevention of cancer, heart disease and diabetes.

Additionally, cooked mushrooms are a concentrated source of potassium, which helps lower blood pressure. Many varieties of mushrooms are rich in selenium, an antioxidant mineral with anticancer properties.

selection and storage

All supermarkets stock white button mushrooms, but many have expanded their selection to include more exotic varieties including shiitake, morel, chanterelle, enoki, oyster, dried Chinese wood-ear and portobello.

Mushrooms like cool, humid, circulating air and need to be stored in a paper bag or ventilated container in the refrigerator, but not in the crisper drawer. Mushrooms last a couple of days, but can still be used in cooking after they've turned brown.

preparation and serving tips

To clean, use a mushroom brush or wipe with a damp cloth but do not submerge in water. Mushrooms cook quickly; overcooking makes them rubbery and tough. Portobello mushrooms are good for grilling and can be substituted for meat in stir-fries, burgers and other dishes.

nutrients per serving:

Mushrooms
½ cup cooked

Calories 22 **Protein** 2g **Total Fat** 1g **Saturated Fat** 0g
Cholesterol 0mg **Carbohydrate** 4g **Dietary Fiber** 2g
Sodium 0mg **Potassium** 278mg **Calcium** 5mg, **Iron** 1.4mg
Vitamin D 16.4 IU **Selenium** 9mcg **Niacin** 3.5mg **Riboflavin** 0.2mg

veggie-stuffed portobello mushrooms

4 large portobello mushrooms
(1¼ to 1½ pounds)
Nonstick cooking spray
2 teaspoons olive oil
1 cup chopped green or red bell
pepper
⅓ cup sliced shallots or chopped onion
2 cloves garlic, minced
1 cup chopped zucchini or summer
squash
½ teaspoon salt
¼ teaspoon black pepper
1 cup panko bread crumbs or toasted
fresh bread crumbs
1 cup (4 ounces) shredded reduced-
fat sharp Cheddar or mozzarella
cheese

nutrients per serving:

Calories 198
Calories from Fat 32%
Protein 11g
Carbohydrate 24g
Fiber 4g

Total Fat 7g
Saturated Fat 3g
Cholesterol 15mg
Sodium 510mg

1. Preheat broiler. Line baking sheet with foil. Gently remove mushroom stems; chop and set aside. Scrape off and discard brown gills from mushroom caps with spoon; place caps top side up on prepared baking sheet. Spray with cooking spray. Broil 4 to 5 inches from heat source 5 minutes or until tender.

2. Meanwhile, heat oil in large nonstick skillet over medium-high heat. Add bell pepper, shallots and garlic; cook and stir 5 minutes or until bell peppers begin to brown. Stir in zucchini, chopped mushroom stems, salt and black pepper; cook and stir 3 to 4 minutes or until vegetables are tender. Remove from heat; cool 5 minutes. Stir in bread crumbs and cheese.

3. Turn mushroom caps over. Mound vegetable mixture into caps. Broil 2 to 3 minutes or until golden brown and cheese is melted.   *Makes 4 servings*

Nectarines

Named for their sweet and juicy nectar, nectarines are the perfect low-calorie treat to satisfy a sweet tooth.

benefits

For only 60 calories, you get a healthy dose of soluble and insoluble fiber from a medium nectarine. Soluble fiber found in the flesh helps lower blood cholesterol levels while insoluble fiber in the skin helps prevent constipation. This delicious cousin of the peach is especially high in beta-carotene, an antioxidant that is converted to vitamin A by the body. The flesh is also rich in phytonutrients that help protect against cancer. Nectarines are a rich source of potassium, an important mineral in blood pressure control.

selection and storage

Nectarines look like a peach without the fuzz, but white nectarines with lighter skin and flesh are also available. Nectarines are at their best from midspring to early fall. Choose nectarines that are firm yet give slightly to the touch. Avoid any with bruises or blemishes as well as those that are hard or overly green. Slightly underripe nectarines will ripen at room temperature within a couple of days. Refrigerate to help slow ripening and use within five days.

preparation and serving tips

A ripe nectarine is a juicy treat, whether eaten out of hand or cut into slices. They make a delicious addition to salads and can be used in a variety of fresh or cooked desserts. The flesh will darken when exposed to air, so be sure to sprinkle with lemon juice to prevent browning when serving fresh in salads or desserts.

nutrients per serving:

Nectarine 1 medium

Calories 62
Protein 2g
Total Fat 0g
Saturated Fat 0g
Cholesterol 0mg
Carbohydrate 15g
Dietary Fiber 2.5g
Sodium 0mg
Potassium 285mg
Calcium 9mg
Iron 0.4mg
Vitamin A 471 IU
Vitamin C 8mg
Folate 7mcg

summertime fruit medley

2 large ripe peaches, peeled and sliced
2 large ripe nectarines, sliced
1 large ripe mango, peeled and cut
    into 1-inch chunks
1 cup blueberries
2 cups orange juice
¼ cup amaretto *or* ½ teaspoon
    almond extract
2 tablespoons sugar

1. Combine peaches, nectarines, mango and blueberries in large bowl.

2. Whisk orange juice, amaretto and sugar in small bowl until sugar is dissolved. Pour over fruit mixture; toss to coat. Marinate at room temperature 1 hour, stirring occasionally.

Makes 8 servings

nutrients per serving:

Calories 112
Calories from Fat 2%
Protein 1g
Carbohydrate 24g
Fiber 2g

Total Fat <1g
Saturated Fat <1g
Cholesterol 0mg
Sodium 8mg

Oats

Oats, the classic breakfast staple, are full of whole grain goodness. All forms of oats—instant, quick, old-fashioned and steel cut—are considered whole grains because they contain the fiber-rich bran layer.

benefits

Oats are rich in soluble fiber and a good source of protein, which makes them perfect for breakfast because they leave you feeling full longer. Eating oatmeal for breakfast can also help you meet the USDA's recommendation in the Dietary Guidelines to make at least half of the grains you eat whole grains. Oats are also a source of calcium, iron, manganese and niacin.

selection and storage

Cooking time and texture are the only differences among the varieties of oats. Chewy steel-cut oats are whole oats sliced into thick pieces and take about 20 minutes to cook. Old-fashioned oats are steamed and flattened and take about 5 minutes to cook. Quick oats are cut into smaller pieces before being rolled and cook in about a minute. Instant oats are precooked so it takes only boiling water to reconstitute them. Instant oats may have added sodium and flavored versions also have added sugar. Store in a dark, dry location in an airtight container for up to a year.

preparation and serving tips

Oats are most commonly used as breakfast cereal or to make cookies, but they can also be used to boost fiber in many dishes, including meat loaves, burgers and fish patties. Grind oats in a blender or food processor and use to thicken soups or sauces, or as a partial substitute for flour in baked goods.

nutrients per serving:

Oats
½ cup cooked

Calories 83 **Protein** 3g **Total Fat** 2g **Saturated Fat** 0g
Cholesterol 0mg **Carbohydrate** 14g **Dietary Fiber** 2g
Sodium 5mg **Potassium** 80mg **Calcium** 11mg **Iron** 1.1mg
Magnesium 32mg **Manganese** 0.7mg **Niacin** 0.3mg

chocolate chip-cherry oatmeal cookies

⅔ cup sugar
⅓ cup canola oil
¼ cup cholesterol-free egg substitute
1 teaspoon vanilla
¾ cup all-purpose flour
½ teaspoon baking soda
½ teaspoon ground cinnamon
⅛ teaspoon salt
1½ cups quick oats
¼ cup mini semisweet chocolate chips
½ cup dried cherries, raisins or
    cranberries

1. Preheat oven to 325°F. Spray cookie sheets with nonstick cooking spray.

2. Beat sugar, oil, egg substitute and vanilla in large bowl with electric mixer at medium speed until well blended. Add flour, baking soda, cinnamon and salt; beat until smooth. Stir in oats, chocolate chips and cherries.

3. Place slightly rounded teaspoonfuls of dough about 2 inches apart on prepared cookie sheets. Bake 7 minutes (cookies will not brown). Cool cookies 2 minutes on cookie sheets. Remove to wire rack to cool completely.

Makes 24 servings (2 cookies per serving)

nutrients per serving:

Calories 103
Calories from Fat 34%
Protein 1g
Carbohydrate 16g
Fiber 1g
Total Fat 4g
Saturated Fat <1g
Cholesterol 0mg
Sodium 45mg

Okra

Popular in Cajun gumbo and other Southern recipes, this nutritious edible pod vegetable offers dieters some attractive benefits.

nutrients per serving:

Okra
½ cup cooked

Calories 18
Protein 2g
Total Fat 0g
Saturated Fat 0g
Cholesterol 0mg
Carbohydrate 4g
Dietary Fiber 2g
Sodium 5mg
Potassium 110mg
Calcium 62mg
Iron 0.2mg
Vitamin A 226 IU
Vitamin C 13mg
Folate 37mcg

benefits

Okra is very low in calories, providing less than 20 calories per cooked serving. It is a rich source of soluble fiber, which swells in the stomach and makes you feel full. Okra also contains healthy amounts of vitamins A and C, calcium and folate, nutrients that help reduce the risk for heart disease.

selection and storage

When purchased fresh, okra has green, ridged skin and a tapered, oblong pod. It is usually available from May through October, but can also be found canned and frozen. Look for firm, brightly colored pods less than 4 inches; longer pods may be tough and fibrous. Avoid those that are dull in color, limp or blemished. Store in the refrigerator and use within five days. Rinse canned okra thoroughly to reduce sodium content.

preparation and serving tips

Rinse okra before cooking to remove dirt or residue, then trim the crown end and tip; it can be sliced into small circular sections or cooked whole depending on the recipe. Okra can be prepared in many ways including braised, sautéed and baked. It makes a nice addition to soups and stews because it gives off a thick liquid that thickens the liquid it's cooked in. Okra can also be served as a side dish or mixed in with other vegetables, meat or rice.

new orleans pork gumbo

1 pound pork tenderloin, cut into
    ½-inch pieces
1 tablespoon butter
2 tablespoons all-purpose flour
1 cup water
1 can (16 ounces) stewed tomatoes,
    undrained
1 package (10 ounces) frozen cut okra
1 package (10 ounces) frozen succotash
1 beef bouillon cube
1 teaspoon black pepper
1 teaspoon hot pepper sauce
1 bay leaf

1. Spray large Dutch oven with nonstick cooking spray; heat over medium heat. Add pork; cook and stir 4 minutes or until browned. Remove from Dutch oven.

2. Melt butter in same Dutch oven. Add flour; cook and stir until mixture is dark brown but not burned. Gradually whisk in water until smooth. Add pork and remaining ingredients; bring to a boil. Reduce heat to low; simmer 15 minutes. Remove bay leaf before serving.

Makes 4 servings

nutrients per serving:

Calories 295	**Carbohydrate** 33g	**Saturated Fat** 3g
Calories from Fat 30%	**Fiber** 7g	**Cholesterol** 45mg
Protein 21g	**Total Fat** 10g	**Sodium** 602mg

Onions

Like other members of the allium family, including leeks, shallots and garlic, onions enhance the flavor of any dish without increasing the calorie count, making them a valuable ingredient in any weight-loss diet.

benefits

Onions have an array of health benefits beyond their low-calorie profile. Like garlic, onions help reduce blood clotting and cholesterol levels. They also contain powerful phytonutrients that help improve the integrity of blood vessels and decrease inflammation. One in particular, quercetin, may play a role in preventing colon cancer by inhibiting tumor growth. Onions also contain vitamin C, folate and fiber. The bright green tops of green onions provide vitamin A, which is great for skin and eye health.

selection and storage

Onions are available in many varieties, shapes and colors. Choose firm dry onions with shiny tissue-thin skins. Avoid those that are discolored or have wet spots. Onions keep three to four weeks in a cool, dry, dark location. Do not store them near potatoes, which give off a gas that causes onions to decay. Look for green onions with crisp, unwilted tops and keep them in an open plastic bag in the crisper drawer of the refrigerator.

preparation and serving tips

To minimize tears, refrigerate onions before cutting or slicing. Red and green onions taste great raw; other onions are best cooked to mellow their flavor. Onions sauté wonderfully in a small amount of oil or broth. When cooking with green onions, be sure to trim the roots and remove the outer layer before chopping.

nutrients per serving:

**Onion, white
½ cup raw chopped**

Calories 32
Protein 1g
Total Fat 0g
Saturated Fat 0g
Cholesterol 0mg
Carbohydrate 8g
Dietary Fiber 1.5g
Sodium 0mg
Potassium 115mg
Calcium 18mg
Iron 0.2mg
Chromium 12mcg
Vitamin C 6mg
Folate 15mcg

glazed chicken & vegetable skewers

12 small red or new potatoes, about 1½ inches in diameter (1 pound)
Golden Glaze (recipe follows)
1 pound boneless skinless chicken thighs or breasts, cut into 1-inch pieces
1 yellow or red bell pepper, cut into 1-inch pieces
½ small red onion, cut into 1-inch pieces

1. Place potatoes in large saucepan; cover with water. Bring to a boil over medium heat; cook 15 minutes or until almost tender.

2. Prepare Golden Glaze. Alternately thread chicken, potatoes, bell pepper and onion onto eight 12-inch skewers.* Brush evenly with glaze.

*If using wooden skewers, soak 20 minutes to prevent burning.

3. Prepare grill for direct cooking. Place skewers on grid over medium-high heat. Grill, covered, 14 to 16 minutes or until chicken is cooked through and vegetables are crisp-tender, turning once.

Makes 4 servings

golden glaze

¼ cup apricot or peach preserves
2 tablespoons spicy brown mustard*
2 cloves garlic, minced

Dijon mustard can be substituted. Add ¼ teaspoon hot pepper sauce.

Combine all ingredients in small bowl; mix well.

Makes about ⅓ cup

nutrients per serving:

Calories 272
Calories from Fat 20%
Protein 16g
Carbohydrate 39g
Fiber <1
Total Fat 6g
Saturated Fat g
Cholesterol 46mg
Sodium 153mg

Oranges

Sweet and juicy oranges are perfect for weight-loss diets; they satisfy a craving for sweets and have several health benefits.

nutrients per serving:

Orange, navel 1 medium

Calories 69
Protein 1g
Total Fat 0g
Saturated Fat 0g
Cholesterol 0mg
Carbohydrate 18g
Dietary Fiber 3g
Sodium 0mg
Potassium 230mg
Calcium 60mg
Iron 0.2mg
Vitamin A 346 IU
Vitamin C 83mg
Folate 48mcg

benefits

Oranges are known for containing vitamin C, an antioxidant that provides immune protection; one orange provides 130 percent of the daily requirement. But oranges also provide many other nutrients, including folate, potassium and several phytonutrients. Even the fibrous white membranes inside the orange have health benefits; they help curb appetite and suppress hunger levels after eating.

selection and storage

Oranges are one of the few fruits abundant in winter. California navel oranges are the most popular for eating, while Valencias, grown primarily in Florida, are the premier juice producing oranges. Mandarin oranges are small and sweet with thin skins and easily sectioned segments; these are also available canned. For all varieties, select firm fruit that's heavy for its size, which indicates juiciness. Fruit with a green color or blemishes are perfectly fine. Most varieties will keep for two weeks in the refrigerator. Orange juice is available freshly squeezed and from or not from concentrate; just be sure it is 100 percent juice with no added sugar.

preparation and serving tips

Fresh oranges are wonderful for eating out of hand. Orange juice has many uses beyond breakfast. Use it to make marinades or nonfat sauces and dressings, or blend with a banana and low-fat yogurt for a delicious smoothie.

citrus tapioca pudding

- 2 navel oranges, divided
- 2½ cups fat-free (skim) milk
- ⅓ cup sugar
- ¼ cup cholesterol-free egg substitute
- 3 tablespoons tapioca
- ½ teaspoon almond extract
- Ground cinnamon or nutmeg
- Orange slices (optional)

1. Grate peel of one orange into medium saucepan. Add milk, sugar, egg substitute and tapioca; let stand 5 minutes. Bring to a boil over medium heat, stirring constantly. Remove from heat; stir in almond extract. Let stand 20 minutes to cool.

2. Stir well; let cool to room temperature. Cover and refrigerate at least 2 hours.

3. Peel and dice oranges; stir into tapioca mixture. Spoon evenly into eight dessert dishes. Sprinkle each serving with cinnamon; garnish with orange slices, if desired.   *Makes 8 servings*

nutrients per serving:

Calories 89
Calories from Fat 2%
Protein 4g
Carbohydrate 19g
Fiber 1g
Total Fat <1g
Saturated Fat <1g
Cholesterol 1mg
Sodium 50mg

Papaya

This tropical fruit with its golden, smooth skin and shiny black seeds is delightfully sweet and tart, making it a treat to eat. Papaya is not as exotic as it sounds and its nutritional profile makes it worth adding to your diet.

benefits

Often dieters miss out on key nutrients by eating less, which is why it is important to eat concentrated sources of nutrients like papaya. It is bursting with health-promoting nutrients including antioxidant vitamins A and C, which reduce your risk for heart disease and cancer. Papayas also provide a hefty dose of potassium, a mineral that helps control blood pressure, and fiber, which helps you to feel full.

selection and storage

Papaya is pear shaped with smooth skin that's golden when ripe. Look for papaya that feels heavy and gives slightly to pressure. To ripen a green papaya, place it in a paper bag at room temperature. Ripe fruit should be refrigerated and used as soon as possible. Papaya juice may be included in blends with other fruit juices but beware of papaya nectar, which is mostly water with added sugar.

preparation and serving tips

Papaya is delicious raw; simply peel, seed and slice it. The peppery black seeds are typically scooped out and discarded but they are edible and make a crunchy addition to salads. They can also be dried and used like peppercorns. Papaya can also be found cooked in Caribbean chicken or fish dishes. Papayas help to tenderize meats by the action of an enzyme found in the fruit called papain.

nutrients per serving:

Papaya
½ medium

Calories 68 **Protein** 1g **Total Fat** 0g
Saturated Fat 0g **Cholesterol** 0mg **Carbohydrate** 17g **Dietary Fiber** 3g
Sodium 15mg **Potassium** 285mg **Calcium** 31mg **Iron** 0.4mg
Vitamin A 1,492 IU **Vitamin C** 96mg **Folate** 58mcg

morning glory cream fizz

1 banana
1 cup cubed and peeled papaya
1 container (6 ounces) low-fat vanilla yogurt
2 tablespoons fat-free half-and-half or milk
1 tablespoon honey
½ cup cold club soda or sparkling water
Papaya slices (optional)

1. Combine banana, papaya, yogurt, half-and-half and honey in blender; blend until smooth.

2. Gently stir in club soda. Pour into three glasses. Garnish with papaya slices. Serve immediately.

Makes 3 servings

nutrients per serving:

Calories 140
Calories from Fat 7%
Protein 4g
Carbohydrate 29g
Fiber 2g
Total Fat 1g
Saturated Fat 1g
Cholesterol 5mg
Sodium 65mg

Parsnips

Welcome parsnips into your diet plan. This sweet, fibrous root vegetable looks like a white carrot and can be used like one, too.

benefits

Parsnips are high in soluble fiber, which absorbs water as it moves through the body and provides a feeling of fullness. Parsnips also contain folate, a B vitamin that plays a role in reducing heart disease, along with an abundance of potassium, which helps control blood pressure.

selection and storage

Parsnips are available year-round in some places but are widely available during winter and early spring. Choose small- to medium-size parsnips; they'll be more tender. The roots should not be small or shriveled and the skin should be smooth and firm. Clip off any greens after purchasing and store in a loosely closed plastic bag in the crisper drawer of the refrigerator for up to two weeks.

preparation and serving tips

Scrub parsnips well before using and trim off the ends. Scrape or peel a thin layer of skin before or after cooking. The most flavorful way to enjoy parsnips is to cut them into chunks, coat them with a little olive oil and roast them; for extra color, flavor and nutrients, add some carrots, too. Parsnips are often enjoyed as a substitute for potatoes. Serve them whole, cut up or puréed like mashed potatoes. Parsnips work great in soups and stews—just add them near the end of cooking time so that they don't overcook and become mushy.

nutrients per serving:

Parsnips
½ cup cooked

Calories 55
Protein 1g
Total Fat 0g
Saturated Fat 0g
Cholesterol 0mg
Carbohydrate 13g
Dietary Fiber 3g
Sodium 10mg
Potassium 285mg
Calcium 29mg
Iron 0.5mg
Vitamin C 10mg
Folate 45mcg

glazed parsnips and carrots

1 pound parsnips (2 large or 3 medium)
1 package (8 ounces) baby carrots
1 tablespoon canola oil
   Salt and black pepper
¼ cup orange juice
1 tablespoon butter
1 tablespoon honey
⅛ teaspoon ground ginger

1. Preheat oven to 425°F. Peel parsnips; cut into pieces the size of carrots.

2. Spread vegetables in shallow baking pan. Drizzle with oil and season with salt and pepper; toss to coat. Bake 30 to 35 minutes or until fork-tender.

3. Combine orange juice, butter, honey and ginger in large skillet. Add vegetables; cook and stir over high heat 1 to 2 minutes or until butter is melted and vegetables are glazed. *Makes 6 servings*

Pasta

While many dieters shun this comfort food, there's no need. Whole wheat pasta can be a regular part of your weight-loss plan as long as you forgo the creamy sauces and heavy meats.

benefits

The fiber and protein found in whole wheat (or whole grain) pasta make it more filling and satisfying than its white counterpart. Whole wheat pasta is superior to white pasta because it is rich in minerals that are usually lost when grains are refined.

selection and storage

To simplify your pasta choices, look for products labeled as whole wheat or whole grain. These are widely available in all supermarkets. Whole wheat pasta is darker in color and tends to have a chewier texture than white varieties. Whole grain pastas are made with a mix of nutrient-rich ingredients including legumes, oats, barley and flax. Store dried pasta at room temperature for several months.

preparation and serving tips

Pasta is best cooked until al dente (tender yet chewy). The cook time varies with the shape of the pasta so check the package. Drain immediately and do not rinse. To prevent sticking, immediately toss with olive oil or a low-fat vegetable sauce. For a meatless meal, toss some whole wheat pasta with your favorite beans and vegetables, drizzle with olive oil and add a squeeze of lemon and some fresh herbs.

nutrients per serving:

Pasta, whole wheat
½ cup cooked

Calories 87 **Protein** 3.5g **Total Fat** 0g **Saturated Fat** 0g
Cholesterol 0mg **Carbohydrate** 19g **Dietary Fiber** 3g
Sodium 0mg **Potassium** 30mg **Calcium** 10mg **Iron** 0.7mg
Vitamin A 2 IU **Folate** 4mcg

Pea Pods

Pea pods are delightfully crunchy raw as a low-calorie snack and make a tasty addition when cooked in your favorite stir-fry.

nutrients per serving:

Peas, snow peas, sugar snap peas
½ cup raw

Calories 13
Protein 1g
Total Fat 0g
Saturated Fat 0g
Cholesterol 0mg
Carbohydrate 2.5g
Dietary Fiber 1g
Sodium 1.5mg
Potassium 63mg
Calcium 13.5mg
Iron 0.7mg
Vitamin A 343 IU
Vitamin C 18.9mg
Folate 13.3mcg

benefits

Pea pods contain a mix of insoluble and soluble fibers, so they keep your digestive system healthy while fighting off hunger. Pea pods also have more protein than many vegetables, which makes them even more satisfying for dieters. Additionally, they are a good source of vitamin C and iron, which help strengthen the immune system.

selection and storage

Fresh snow peas (Chinese pea pods) are available year-round. Look for small, shiny, flat pods as they're the sweetest and most tender. Sugar snap peas have edible pods like snow peas, but are sweet like green peas. Select those with plump, bright green pods. Many supermarkets sell packaged pea pods.

When you can't get fresh pea pods, try frozen. They work wonderfully in cooking.

preparation and serving tips

Snow peas and sugar snap peas just need washing and trimming before cooking or eating raw. Raw sugar snap peas are great to munch on and go well with any low-fat dip. Snow peas are the perfect addition to your favorite stir-fry dish; cook only a few minutes to keep them crisp. Sugar snap peas can also be lightly steamed and served as a side dish.

Peaches

Nothing beats the juicy sweetness of a ripe peach.

benefits

Peaches aid your weight-loss efforts by supplying the form of fiber that swells in the body, filling you up and leaving you satisfied. Fresh peaches are a good source of a few nutrients, including antioxidants beta-carotene and vitamin C; beta-carotene helps support the immune system and vitamin C helps ward off infections.

selection and storage

Fresh peaches are available May through October. The velvety skins can range from golden red to creamy pink with flesh that is bright orange to white. Look for fragrant fruit that give slightly to pressure. Be cautious of soft spots, as peaches bruise easily. Place them in a paper bag with an apple to speed up ripening. Once ripe, they will last in the refrigerator for up to five days. When fresh peaches aren't available, try frozen, canned or dried peaches. To keep calories low, look for canned peaches in water or juice, and frozen or dried peaches without added sugar.

preparation and serving tips

Rinse fresh peaches and enjoy with the peel for more fiber. Peaches can be enjoyed on their own, in fruit salads, salsas and smoothies. They also work well cooked with meat and poultry. Try grilling or broiling fresh peach halves with a touch of cinnamon or nutmeg for dessert.

nutrients per serving:

Peach
1 medium

Calories 58 *Protein* 1g *Total Fat* 0g *Saturated Fat* 0g
Cholesterol 0mg *Carbohydrate* 14g *Dietary Fiber* 2g
Sodium 0mg *Potassium* 285mg *Calcium* 9mg *Iron* 0.4mg
Vitamin A 489 IU *Vitamin C* 10mg *Folate* 6mcg

chicken, peach and cabbage salad

nutrients per serving:

Calories 154
Calories from Fat 12%
Protein 23g
Carbohydrate 10g
Fiber 2g
Total Fat 2g
Saturated Fat <1g
Cholesterol 54mg
Sodium 174mg

1½ **cups diced cooked chicken breast, chilled**
1 **cup shredded red cabbage**
1 **medium ripe peach, peeled, pitted and cut into 1-inch pieces**
1 **stalk celery, diced**
¼ **cup plain nonfat yogurt**
3 **tablespoons peach nectar or orange juice**
¼ **teaspoon curry powder**
⅛ **teaspoon salt**
⅛ **teaspoon black pepper**

1. Combine chicken, cabbage, peach and celery in medium bowl.

2. Whisk yogurt, nectar, curry powder, salt and pepper in small bowl. Add to salad; mix well.

Makes 3 servings

129

Peanuts

Many dieters think peanuts and peanut butter are off limits but that's not necessarily true. In moderation, both provide plenty of flavor and satisfying protein.

nutrients per serving:

Peanuts, dry roasted without salt
1 ounce

Calories 166
Protein 7g
Total Fat 14g
Saturated Fat 2g
Cholesterol 0mg
Carbohydrate 6g
Dietary Fiber 2.5g
Sodium 0mg
Potassium 185mg
Calcium 15mg
Iron 0.6mg
Folate 41mcg
Magnesium 50mg
Vitamin E 2mg

benefits

While peanuts are technically considered a legume, they are a terrific source of protein and have more than any nut. Research shows that peanuts and peanut butter make up for their high calorie count by fighting hunger. One study found that people who ate a carbohydrate-rich snack reduced their hunger for about 30 minutes, while those who ate a snack of peanuts or peanut butter lasted for 2 hours and ate fewer calories throughout the day.

selection and storage

Peanuts are sold both shelled and unshelled. When buying in the shell, look for clean, unbroken shells that do not rattle when shaken. Shelled peanuts are usually roasted and often salted, as well. Choose dry roasted peanuts rather than oil roasted for less fat and calories. Unshelled peanuts can keep for a few months in a cool, dry location but once they're shelled or the container has been opened, store them in the refrigerator or freezer for up to three months. Peanut butter is available as natural or blended with added sugar.

preparation and serving tips

Enjoy peanuts as a snack, but keep your portion to about 1 ounce (a small handful). Sprinkle peanuts on salads or stir-fries for added crunch and flavor. Spread peanut butter on apple wedges, crackers or toast.

spicy chicken bundles

- 1 **pound ground chicken or turkey**
- 2 **teaspoons minced fresh ginger**
- 2 **cloves garlic, minced**
- ¼ **teaspoon red pepper flakes**
- 3 **tablespoons soy sauce**
- 1 **tablespoon cornstarch**
- 1 **tablespoon peanut or vegetable oil**
- ⅓ **cup finely chopped water chestnuts**
- ⅓ **cup thinly sliced green onions**
- ¼ **cup chopped peanuts**
- 12 **large lettuce leaves, such as romaine**
  Chinese hot mustard (optional)

1. Combine chicken, ginger, garlic and red pepper flakes in medium bowl. Whisk soy sauce into cornstarch in small bowl until smooth.

2. Heat oil in wok or large skillet over medium-high heat. Add chicken mixture; cook and stir 2 to 3 minutes or until chicken is cooked through.

3. Add soy sauce mixture; cook and stir 30 seconds or until sauce boils and thickens. Add water chestnuts, green onions and peanuts; cook until heated through.*

4. Divide filling evenly among lettuce leaves; roll up to enclose filling. Serve with hot mustard, if desired.

Makes 12 servings

*Filling may be made ahead to this point; cover and refrigerate up to 4 hours. Reheat until warm; proceed as directed in step 4.

nutrients per serving:

Calories 90
Calories from Fat 55%
Protein 8g
Carbohydrate 3g
Fiber 1g

Total Fat 6g
Saturated Fat 2g
Cholesterol 35mg
Sodium 25mg

Pears

Their sweet flavor and slightly crunchy texture, along with their great nutrition profile, make pears a fruit to include in any diet.

benefits

Pears have more fiber than any other fruit except berries, so they work well with weight-loss efforts. Their soluble fiber keeps you satisfied longer and the sweet taste helps you forgo less nutritious snacks. Pears are a good source of heart-healthy nutrients including potassium, vitamin C and folate.

selection and storage

There are several widely available varieties of pears. Juicy Bartletts are the most common and are also available canned. Anjou pears, which are firmer and not quite as sweet, and crunchy Boscs, which have elongated necks and russet coloring, are great all-purpose pears. Comice pears are the sweetest variety. Pears ripen from the inside out, so it's best to buy them firm but not rock hard. Ripen them on the counter or in a ventilated paper bag, but do not pile them up or they'll bruise. Choose canned pears packed in juice rather than syrup and be aware that they have less fiber than fresh because they're peeled.

preparation and serving tips

Firm pears work well in salads or for cooking. Ripe pears are great mixed with nonfat yogurt and cereal for breakfast. Bartlett and Bosc pears are good for cooking; try poaching them in wine or juice or sautéing with a sprinkle of brown sugar.

nutrients per serving:

Pears
1 medium

Calories 103 **Protein** 1g **Total Fat** 0g
Saturated Fat 0g **Cholesterol** 0mg
Carbohydrate 28g **Dietary Fiber** 5.5g
Sodium 0mg **Potassium** 210mg
Calcium 16mg **Iron** 0.3mg
Vitamin A 41 IU **Vitamin C** 8mg
Folate 12mcg

autumn fruit crisp

⅓ cup old-fashioned oats
¼ cup packed brown sugar
2 tablespoons whole wheat flour
½ teaspoon ground cinnamon
2 tablespoons cold margarine or butter, cut into small pieces
2 baking apples,* peeled and sliced (1 pound)
1 pear, peeled and sliced (8 ounces)

*Choose Rome or Winesap apples.

1. Preheat oven to 350°F. Spray 8-inch square baking dish with nonstick cooking spray.

2. Combine oats, brown sugar, flour and cinnamon in medium bowl; mix well. Cut in margarine with pastry blender or two knives until mixture resembles coarse crumbs.

3. Place apples and pears in baking dish; sprinkle with oat mixture. Bake 35 minutes or until topping is lightly browned and fruit is tender.   *Makes 6 servings*

nutrients per serving:

Calories 134
Calories from Fat 28%
Protein 1g
Carbohydrate 24g
Fiber 3g
Total Fat 4g
Saturated Fat 3g
Cholesterol 10mg
Sodium 32mg

Pineapple

Eating sweet, tart and juicy pineapple is a low-calorie way to satisfy your sweet tooth.

benefits

Pineapple is filling, satisfying and rather nutritious. One cup exceeds a day's recommended amount of manganese, one of many bone-strengthening minerals that may also be important for energy production. A serving of pineapple also provides a decent amount of folate, plus more than one third of your recommended intake of vitamin C, increasing your resistance to colds, flu and other infectious diseases. Fresh raw pineapple contains an enzyme called bromelain that aids digestion and helps prevent inflammation and swelling.

selection and storage

When choosing pineapple, let your nose be your guide. A ripe pineapple gives off a sweet aroma from its base. Color is not a reliable indicator; ripe pineapples vary in color by variety. Choose a large pineapple that yields to slight pressure and feels heavy for its size, indicating juiciness and a lot of pulp. Once a pineapple is picked, it will not ripen further. Canned pineapple is

available; be sure to select varieties packed in juice or water, not syrup.

preparation and serving tips

Preparing a pineapple is not as scary it looks. Cut off the bottom and top, then peel the outside using a sharp knife. Remove any remaining eyes. Cut into quarters and remove the core from each quarter, then cut into slices. Use pineapple in fruit salad or skewer and grill it with your favorite meat.

nutrients per serving:

Pineapple
½ cup

Calories 41 **Protein** 1g
Total Fat 0g *Saturated Fat* 0g
Cholesterol 0mg *Carbohydrate* 11g
Dietary Fiber 1g *Sodium* 0mg
Potassium 90mg *Calcium* 11mg
Iron 0.2mg *Manganese* 0.8mg
Vitamin C 39mg *Folate* 15mcg

sweet pineapple cream fruit dip

- **1 can (8 ounces) crushed pineapple in juice**
- **¼ cup whipped light cream cheese**
- **¼ cup fat-free sour cream**
- **3 tablespoons measure-for-measure sugar substitute**
- **Fresh fruit (optional)**

1. Place pineapple in a fine-mesh strainer. Using the back of a spoon, press down firmly to release excess liquid.

2. Combine pineapple, cream cheese, sour cream and sugar substitute in small bowl.

3. Serve immediately with fruit or cover with plastic wrap and refrigerate until ready to serve (up to 24 hours).

Makes 4 servings

nutrients per serving:

Calories 79
Calories from Fat 24%
Protein 3g
Carbohydrate 14g
Fiber <1g
Total Fat 2g
Saturated Fat 2g
Cholesterol 10mg
Sodium 88mg

Plums

Few fruits come in such a spectrum of colors as the sweet and juicy plum; there are more than 100 varieties in the United States alone.

benefits

Plums and prunes (their dried counterparts) are richly colored, indicating they are full of plant pigments called phenols. Phenols, which are antioxidants, protect the vital fat found in cell membranes, brain matter and the fats circulating in the bloodstream. Eating a couple of plums will give you a fair dose of vitamins A and C, potassium and fiber—nutrients that help protect your cells, keep your heart healthy and boost immunity.

selection and storage

Plums are a summer fruit with a long season from May through October. Some plums cling to their pits while others have "free" stones (pits). Plum skins come in a rainbow of colors: red, purple, black, green, blue and even yellow. The flesh varies, too, and can be yellow, orange, green or red. Look for plump fruit with a bright or deep color. If they yield to gentle palm pressure, they're ripe. Once slightly soft, plums should be eaten or refrigerated.

preparation and serving tips

Like many fruits, plums taste sweetest at room temperature. Plums can be added to fruit salads, baked goods, compotes, puddings or meat dishes. They can also be made into butters, jams, purées or sauces. Puréed dried plums (prunes) make a fabulous fat substitute in recipes for quick breads, muffins and other baked goods. Not only do they substantially reduce calories, they also boost the nutrition content.

nutrients per serving:

Plum
1 medium

Calories 30 **Protein** <1g **Total Fat** 0g **Saturated Fat** 0g
Cholesterol 0mg **Carbohydrate** 7g **Dietary Fiber** 1g
Sodium 0mg **Potassium** 105mg **Calcium** 4mg **Iron** 0.1mg
Vitamin A 228 IU **Vitamin C** 6mg **Folate** 3mcg

Pomegranates

It may take time remove the edible seeds from this nutrient-packed fruit, but the tasty results are worth the effort.

nutrients per serving:

Pomegranate Seeds (Arils)
½ cup raw

Calories 72
Protein 1g
Total Fat 1g
Saturated Fat 0g
Cholesterol 0mg
Carbohydrate 16g
Dietary Fiber 3.5g
Sodium 0mg
Potassium 205mg
Calcium 9mg
Iron 0.3mg
Vitamin C 9mg
Folate 33mcg

benefits

Don't be intimidated by their large size—pomegranates are great for dieters because the juicy seeds called arils are full of fiber yet low in calories. Pomegranate juice is nutritious as well, but does not contain any fiber. Both the seeds and the juice are rich in disease-fighting antioxidants that may help reduce artery-clogging plaque by lowering levels of LDL "bad" cholesterol. Pomegranates are rich in potassium, a mineral that plays an important role in blood pressure control.

selection and storage

Pomegranates are at their best in late fall and early winter. Choose pomegranates with unblemished, bright deep red skin that feel heavy for their size. Store in a cool, dark place for up to one month or refrigerate for up to two months. Once cut, the seeds can be refrigerated for about three days or frozen for later use. Pomegranate juice is available in bottles or as concentrate.

preparation and serving tips

Cut pomegranates in half and pry out the seeds, removing the light-colored membrane. For easier removal, soak cut sections of pomegranate in a bowl of water to loosen the seeds. Enjoy the crunchy seeds on their own or use them as a salad topper. To get fresh juice, squeeze a pomegranate half on a juicer or purée the seeds in a food processor and strain the juice. The juice is great in marinades and sauces.

Pork Tenderloin

Chicken isn't the only meat that can fit into a weight-loss plan; make pork tenderloin a regular part of your diet. It is comparable to skinless chicken breasts in both calories and fat.

benefits

The lean protein in pork tenderloin may aid in weight loss. Research published in the journal *Obesity* found that women on a reduced-calorie diet who increased their daily protein intake to 30 percent of calories, including 6 ounces of lean pork, maintained more than double the amount of lean tissue as those who ate less protein and also reported feeling more satisfied. Pork tenderloin has less cholesterol than chicken breasts and more nutrients, providing more than 20 percent of the recommended daily thiamin, niacin, riboflavin, vitamin B6, phosphorus and protein and at least 10 percent of potassium.

nutrients per serving:

Pork Tenderloin
3 ounces roasted

Calories 125 **Protein** 22g **Total Fat** 3.5g **Saturated Fat** 1g **Cholesterol** 62mg **Carbohydrate** <1g **Dietary Fiber** 0g **Sodium** 50mg **Potassium** 355mg **Thiamin** 0.8mg **Riboflavin** 0.3mg **Niacin** 6.3mg **Vitamin B-6** 0.6mg **Phosphorus** 225mg

selection and storage

Four ounces of raw tenderloin yields a 3-ounce cooked serving. Store packaged pork tenderloin in the refrigerator for up to four days or wrap well and freeze for up to six months.

preparation and serving tips

Pork tenderloin makes an elegant entrée for a dinner party but also can easily be roasted or grilled for a quick meal. It has a mild flavor, so it's best when prepared with a spice rub, marinade, stuffing or flavorful sauce. To keep the tenderloin juicy, be careful not to overcook it. A meat thermometer inserted into the thickest part of the meat should reach a temperature of 160°F for medium doneness.

Calories 309
Calories from Fat 22%
Protein 22g

Carbohydrate 39g
Fiber 3g
Total Fat 7g

Saturated Fat 4g
Cholesterol 71mg
Sodium 565mg

pork and sweet potato skillet

1 tablespoon plus 1 teaspoon
    butter, divided
¾ **pound pork tenderloin, cut
    into 1-inch cubes**
¼ **teaspoon salt**
⅛ **teaspoon black pepper**
2 **medium sweet potatoes, peeled
    and cut into ½-inch pieces
    (about 2 cups)**
1 **small onion, sliced**
¼ **pound reduced-fat smoked turkey
    sausage, halved lengthwise
    and cut into ½-inch pieces**
1 **small green or red apple, cored
    and cut into ½-inch pieces**
½ **cup sweet and sour sauce**
2 **tablespoons chopped fresh parsley
    (optional)**

1. Melt 1 teaspoon butter in large skillet over medium-high heat. Add pork; cook and stir 2 to 3 minutes or until pork is no longer pink. Season with salt and pepper. Remove from skillet.

2. Melt remaining 1 tablespoon butter in same skillet over medium-low heat. Add potatoes and onion; cover and cook 8 to 10 minutes or until tender, stirring occasionally.

3. Add pork, sausage, apple and sweet and sour sauce; cook and stir until heated through. Garnish with parsley.

Makes 4 servings

Potatoes

Potatoes are not the first food that comes to mind when you think "diet," but they can be part of your healthy meal plan.

nutrients per serving:

Potato
1 medium baked

Calories 161
Protein 4g
Total Fat 0g
Saturated Fat 0g
Cholesterol 0mg
Carbohydrate 37g
Dietary Fiber 4g
Sodium 15mg
Potassium 925mg
Calcium 26mg
Iron 1.9mg
Vitamin A 17 IU
Vitamin C 17mg
Folate 48mcg

benefits

It's not the carbohydrates in potatoes that sabotage weight-loss efforts—it's the oil they're fried in or the heavy toppings that cause calories and fat to get out of hand. On their own, potatoes are great for dieters; they're moderate in calories, rich in vitamin C and potassium and loaded with a mix of soluble and insoluble fibers, which helps to keep the digestive tract functioning and slow down digestion so you feel full longer. Be sure to eat the skin, which contains most of the fiber.

selection and storage

There are hundreds of varieties of potatoes. Many are all-purpose, but russets are best for baking while new potatoes are suited for boiling. Choose potatoes that are firm with no soft or dark spots. Store potatoes in a cool, dry, dark and ventilated location, away from onions. Mature potatoes keep for several weeks; new potatoes only keep one week.

preparation and serving tips

Just before cooking, scrub potatoes well with a vegetable brush and cut out sprout buds and bad spots. Prick the skin all over with a fork before cooking for a fluffier potato. Baking a potato takes about an hour in the oven, but only 5 minutes in a microwave. Top with nonfat yogurt and sprinkle with chopped dill or green onions for a healthy version of a loaded baked potato. For lower-calorie fries, toss thin-cut potatoes with olive oil, season with salt and pepper and roast in a 400°F oven for about 30 minutes.

cheesy potato skins

- 2 tablespoons grated Parmesan cheese
- 3 cloves garlic, minced
- 2 teaspoons dried rosemary
- ½ teaspoon salt
- ¼ teaspoon black pepper
- 4 baked potatoes
- 2 egg whites, lightly beaten
- ½ cup (2 ounces) shredded part-skim mozzarella cheese

1. Preheat oven to 400°F. Combine Parmesan cheese, garlic, rosemary, salt and pepper in small bowl; set aside.

2. Cut potatoes lengthwise into quarters. Remove and discard pulp, leaving ¼-inch-thick shells.

3. Place shells on baking sheet. Brush with egg whites; sprinkle with Parmesan cheese mixture. Bake 20 minutes.

4. Sprinkle with mozzarella cheese; bake until melted.   *Makes 8 servings*

nutrients per serving:

Calories 90
Calories from Fat 17%
Protein 5g
Carbohydrate 14g
Fiber 2g
Total Fat 2g
Saturated Fat 1g
Cholesterol 5mg
Sodium 215mg

Pumpkin

Not just for Halloween or Thanksgiving, pumpkin, a type of winter squash, has a great taste that lends itself well to a variety of dishes.

benefits

Pumpkin is a good low-calorie source of nutrients, including iron, potassium and fiber. Its bright orange color indicates it is an excellent source of beta-carotene. Research shows that people who eat a diet rich in beta-carotene are less likely to develop certain cancers.

selection and storage

Leave large pumpkins for jack-o'-lanterns as they tend to be tough and stringy and try smaller sugar pumpkins instead. Look for a deep orange pumpkin that is free of cracks or soft spots. A whole pumpkin keeps well for up to one month if stored in a cool, dry spot. Once cut, wrap the pumpkin and refrigerate for about a week. Canned pumpkin is available year-round and is as nutritious as fresh.

preparation and serving tips

To prepare a fresh pumpkin, wash off any dirt, cut away the tough skin with a knife or a vegetable peeler and remove the seeds. Slice, dice or cut the flesh into chunks; then steam, boil or microwave until tender. Purée in a blender for a creamy, savory soup. Besides pumpkin pie, it can be used to make delicious moist cookies or bars and works well as a pudding or custard. Pumpkin is often used to replace the fat in recipes for quick breads, muffins, pancakes, brownies and other desserts.

nutrients per serving:

Pumpkin
½ cup cooked

Calories 24 **Protein** 1g *Total Fat* 0g *Saturated Fat* 0g
Cholesterol 0mg *Carbohydrate* 6g *Dietary Fiber* 1.5g
Sodium 0mg *Potassium* 280mg *Calcium* 18mg **Iron** 0.7mg
Vitamin A 6,115 IU **Vitamin C** 6mg *Folate* 11mcg

spicy pumpkin soup with green chile swirl

- **1 can (4 ounces) diced green chiles**
- **¼ cup reduced-fat sour cream**
- **¼ cup fresh cilantro leaves**
- **1 can (15 ounces) solid-pack pumpkin**
- **1 can (about 14 ounces) fat-free reduced-sodium chicken or vegetable broth**
- **½ cup water**
- **1 teaspoon ground cumin**
- **½ teaspoon chili powder**
- **¼ teaspoon garlic powder**
- **⅛ teaspoon ground red pepper (optional)**

1. Combine chiles, sour cream and cilantro in food processor or blender; process until smooth.

2. Combine pumpkin, broth, water, cumin, chili powder, garlic powder and red pepper, if desired, in medium saucepan.

Stir in ¼ cup green chile mixture. Bring to a boil; reduce heat to medium. Simmer 5 minutes, stirring occasionally.

3. Pour into serving bowls. Top each serving with small dollops of remaining green chile mixture. Run tip of spoon through dollops to swirl.

Makes 4 servings

nutrients per serving:

Calories 72
Calories from Fat 17%
Protein 4g
Carbohydrate 12g
Fiber 4g

Total Fat 1g
Saturated Fat <1g
Cholesterol 5mg
Sodium 276mg

Quinoa

Pronounced "KEEN-wah," this ancient grain was sacred to the Incas. It is a rich and balanced source of nutrients and contains a high amount of protein, making it ideal for dieters.

benefits

The high protein content of quinoa makes it great for dieters, providing longer lasting energy to help manage hunger. Quinoa is also higher in unsaturated fats and lower in carbohydrates than most grains. It's an excellent source of various minerals, including iron, magnesium, potassium, phosphorus and zinc. Plus, it provides fiber, making it an all-around healthy choice.

selection and storage

Quinoa is becoming more popular and is now available in many supermarkets near the rice and other grains. It has a tiny beaded shape and is available in various colors such as red, black and ivory. Dry quinoa should be stored in an airtight container in a cool, dry place or in the refrigerator. Quinoa is also available ground into flour and in several forms of pasta.

preparation and serving tips

Rinse quinoa before cooking. Combine one part quinoa to two parts water or broth in a medium or large saucepan. Allow for room as it will expand to four times its original volume when cooked. Bring to a simmer and then reduce to low. Cover and cook for about 30 minutes; fluff with a fork. Quinoa has a delicate flavor and can be substituted for grains in almost any recipe; it works well in salads and side dishes and can be used as a substitute for oatmeal.

nutrients per serving:

Quinoa
½ cup cooked

Calories 111
Protein 4g
Total Fat 2g
Saturated Fat 0g
Cholesterol 0mg
Carbohydrate 20g
Dietary Fiber 2.5g
Sodium 6mg
Potassium 160mg
Iron 1.4mg
Zinc 1mg
Magnesium 59mg
Phosphorus 141mg
Folate 39mcg

quinoa with roasted vegetables

Nonstick cooking spray
2 medium sweet potatoes, cut into ½-inch-thick slices
1 medium eggplant, peeled and cut into ½-inch cubes
1 medium tomato, cut into wedges
1 large green bell pepper, sliced
1 small onion, cut into wedges
½ teaspoon salt
¼ teaspoon black pepper
¼ teaspoon ground red pepper
1 cup uncooked quinoa
2 cloves garlic, minced
½ teaspoon dried thyme
¼ teaspoon dried marjoram
2 cups water or fat-free reduced-sodium vegetable broth

1. Preheat oven to 450°F. Line large jelly-roll pan with foil; spray with nonstick cooking spray.

2. Arrange sweet potatoes, eggplant, tomato, bell pepper and onion in prepared pan; spray with cooking spray. Sprinkle with salt, black pepper and ground red pepper; toss to coat. Roast 20 to 30 minutes or until vegetables are browned and tender.

3. Meanwhile, place quinoa in fine-mesh strainer; rinse well. Spray medium saucepan with cooking spray; heat over medium heat. Add garlic, thyme and marjoram; cook and stir 1 to 2 minutes. Add quinoa; cook and stir 2 to 3 minutes. Stir in water; bring to a boil over high heat. Reduce heat to low. Cover and simmer 15 to 20 minutes or until water is absorbed and quinoa appears somewhat translucent.

4. Transfer quinoa to large bowl; gently stir in roasted vegetables. *Makes 6 servings*

nutrients per serving:

Calories 193
Calories from Fat 9%
Protein 6g
Carbohydrate 40g
Fiber 6g
Total Fat 2g
Saturated Fat <1g
Cholesterol 0mg
Sodium 194mg

Raspberries

Although raspberries look fragile and exquisite, there's nothing delicate about the flavor and nutrients you get from this tiny member of the rose family.

benefits

Raspberries are almost unrivaled in the amount of fiber they contain and in their antioxidant strength. Low in calories, raspberries provide a whopping 8 grams of fiber per cup, helping to fill you up. The fruit is high in pectin, a form of soluble fiber known to help lower blood cholesterol. Raspberries are also a good source of vitamin C, an antioxidant, and ellagic acid, a phytochemical, both of which help fight against cancer.

selection and storage

Raspberries are fragile and should be handled carefully and eaten soon after purchasing. Look for berries that are brightly colored with no hulls attached. Avoid any that look shriveled or have visible mold. They should be plump, firm and well shaped with a slightly sweet fragrance. Frozen unsweetened raspberries are also available and work well in smoothies and baked goods.

preparation and serving tips

Rinse raspberries under cool water just before serving. For a low-fat dessert, top frozen sorbet or a slice of angel food cake with whole chilled raspberries. Purée fresh or frozen raspberries to create a sweet and tart sauce to top a fruit salad, a slice of low-fat cake, pancakes or waffles. If you're celebrating a special occasion, enjoy a glass of champagne with some chilled ripe raspberries. Raspberries also make a colorful, edible garnish.

nutrients per serving:

Raspberries
½ cup raw

Calories 32 *Protein* 1g *Total Fat* 0g
Saturated Fat 0g *Cholesterol* 0mg
Carbohydrate 7g *Dietary Fiber* 4g
Sodium 0mg *Potassium* 95mg
Calcium 15mg *Iron* 0.4mg
Vitamin A 20 IU *Vitamin C* 16mg
Folate 13mcg

nutrients per serving:

Calories 14
Calories from Fat 0%
Protein <1g
Carbohydrate 3g
Fiber 1g

Total Fat 0g
Saturated Fat <1g
Cholesterol 0mg
Sodium 1mg

frosty raspberry lemon tea

1½ cups ice
 1 cup brewed lemon-flavored
    herbal tea, at room
    temperature
 1 cup water
 ½ cup frozen unsweetened
    raspberries

1. Combine all ingredients in blender; blend until smooth, pulsing as necessary to break up ice.

2. Pour into two tall glasses and serve immediately.

Makes 2 servings

Rosemary

Rosemary's aromatic pinelike scent is associated with flavorful food and good health. Bring any low-calorie dish to life with this fragrant herb.

benefits

Like other herbs and spices, rosemary helps support weight loss by making low-calorie dishes, such as roasted vegetables and lean meats, more flavorful and satisfying. It also brings some important benefits to overall health as you're watching your weight; it stimulates the immune system, increases circulation and improves digestion. In addition, rosemary has been shown to increase blood flow to the head and brain, improving concentration.

selection and storage

Like other herbs, fresh rosemary is best. Look for it at supermarkets and farmers' markets or you can easily grow your own. Once cut, fresh rosemary should be wrapped in damp paper towels and stored in the refrigerator for up to a week. Or leave it out to dry, then remove the leaves and store in a glass jar. Dried rosemary is readily available in the spice section of the supermarket. Store it away from heat and light for up to a year.

preparation and storage tips

Rosemary pairs well with lean meats, including pork, fish, chicken and lamb. Rosemary also works well in herb blends with oregano, thyme and basil; add some olive oil and minced garlic and use as a rub for meats. Rosemary complements roasted potatoes and imparts a wonderful flavor to sautéed eggplant, tomatoes and zucchini.

nutrients per serving:

**Rosemary, fresh
2 tablespoons**

Calories 4 *Protein* 0g
Total Fat 0g *Saturated Fat* 0g
Cholesterol 0mg *Carbohydrate* <1g
Dietary Fiber 0.5g *Sodium* 0mg
Potassium 23mg *Calcium* 11mg
Iron 0.2mg *Vitamin A* 99 IU
Vitamin C 1mg *Folate* 4mcg

nutrients per serving:

Calories 205
Calories from Fat 39%
Protein 25g

Carbohydrate 5g
Fiber <1g
Total Fat 9g

Saturated Fat 3g
Cholesterol 72mg
Sodium 402mg

seared beef tenderloin with horseradish-rosemary cream

- 1 **teaspoon chili powder**
- ½ **teaspoon salt, divided**
- ¼ **teaspoon plus ⅛ teaspoon black pepper, divided**
- 1 **pound beef tenderloin**
- 1 **clove garlic, halved**
  Nonstick cooking spray
- ⅓ **cup fat-free sour cream**
- 3 **tablespoons fat-free (skim) milk**
- 2 **teaspoons reduced-fat mayonnaise**
- 1 **teaspoon prepared horseradish**
- ¼ **teaspoon dried rosemary**

1. Preheat oven to 425°F. Combine chili powder, ¼ teaspoon salt and ¼ teaspoon pepper in small bowl. Rub tenderloin with garlic; sprinkle evenly with seasoning mixture.

2. Spray medium ovenproof skillet with nonstick cooking spray; heat over medium-high heat. Add beef tenderloin; cook 2 minutes on each side.

3. Transfer skillet to oven. Bake 30 minutes or until internal temperature reaches 140°F. Cover and let stand 15 minutes.

4. Meanwhile, combine sour cream, milk, mayonnaise, horseradish, rosemary, remaining ¼ teaspoon salt and ⅛ teaspoon pepper in small bowl; mix well. Cut tenderloin into four pieces. Spoon sauce over each serving.   *Makes 4 servings*

Rye

Rye makes a hearty filling and nutritious bread that is great for sandwiches. It is a cereal grain that contains more fiber than wheat, making it an excellent choice for dieters.

nutrients per serving:

Rye Bread
1 slice

Calories 83
Protein 3g
Total Fat 1g
Saturated Fat 0g
Cholesterol 0mg
Carbohydrate 15g
Dietary Fiber 2g
Sodium 211mg
Potassium 53mg
Calcium 23mg
Iron 0.9mg
Thiamin 0.1mg
Riboflavin 0.1mg
Folate 35mcg

benefits

Rye is particularly rich in insoluble fiber, which binds with water and quickly gives a feeling of fullness and satisfaction. One study found that eating rye products helped dieters consume fewer calories at their next meal. Its fiber also helps keep your digestive system working smoothly. Rye contains powerful phytonutrients that may have anticancer activity equal to or even higher than fruits and vegetables. Compared to whole wheat bread, rye bread contains more iron and B vitamins.

selection and storage

Rye grains may be available whole, cracked or rolled, but are generally ground into flour. Rye flour comes as light rye flour, which has most of the bran (fiber) removed, while dark rye flour retains most of the bran and germ, so it has more fiber and nutrients. Store rye grains in an airtight container in a cool, dry, dark place for several months. Rye bread is available in the bread aisle and bakery of the supermarket.

preparation and serving tips

Rye bread is generally more compact and dense than wheat bread, so it works well for toasting or for sandwiches with hearty and moist fillings. Whole rye should be soaked overnight and will take longer to cook than cracked rye; it can be served like rice in soups, stews and stir-fries.

reuben bites

  24 party rye bread slices
  ½ cup prepared fat-free Thousand
     Island dressing
  6 ounces turkey pastrami, very
     thinly sliced
  1 cup (4 ounces) shredded reduced-
     fat Swiss cheese
  1 cup alfalfa sprouts

1. Preheat oven to 400°F. Arrange bread slices on nonstick baking sheet. Bake 5 minutes or until lightly toasted.

2. Spread 1 teaspoon dressing on each bread slice; top with pastrami, folding to fit bread slices. Sprinkle evenly with cheese.

3. Bake 5 minutes or until heated through. Top evenly with sprouts. Serve immediately.
Makes 12 servings

nutrients per serving:

Calories 142
Calories from Fat 21%
Protein 9g
Carbohydrate 19g
Fiber <1g
Total Fat 3g
Saturated Fat 1g
Cholesterol 15mg
Sodium 516mg

Shellfish

This category of seafood includes any water-dwelling creature that wears its skeleton on the outside like oysters, clams, mussels, lobster, shrimp, crab and scallops.

benefits

All shellfish are lean, high in protein and rich in nutrients, making them a terrific diet food. Weight for weight, they contain more vitamin B_{12} than any other animal protein. Crab and lobster have high calcium counts, good for healthy bones and teeth, as well as copper to help in production of blood cells, connective tissue and nerve fibers. Oysters, scallops and shrimp have an abundance of magnesium for metabolism and bone growth. Shellfish are very low in saturated fat and offer heart-healthy omega-3 fat, which is found almost exclusively in seafood.

selection and storage

Fresh shellfish, whether in the shell or shucked, should smell briny without any hint of fishiness. With the exception of shrimp, scallops and crabmeat, fresh shellfish should be kept alive until ready to cook; never put live shellfish in an airtight container or fresh water as they can suffocate. Fresh shellfish should be eaten within one to two days. Frozen shellfish should be tightly wrapped and should not be covered in ice crystals.

preparation and serving tips

Shellfish is most commonly steamed in the shell but don't overcook or the flesh will be rubbery and tough. Oysters and clams show their freshness by flinching when you squeeze lemon juice on them and should snap shut when tapped. Clams and mussels are done when their shells open. Remove them from the cooking liquid as they open and continue cooking until all are opened. Discard any that do not open. Shellfish can be served as a main course or added to other dishes, such as soups, salads, stews and stir-fries. To keep shellfish low in fat, serve with low-fat dips and sauces such as cocktail sauce, soy sauce and lemon juice.

nutrients per serving:

Shrimp
3 ounces cooked

Calories 101 *Protein* 19g *Total Fat* 2g *Saturated Fat* 0g
Cholesterol 179mg *Carbohydrate* 1g *Dietary Fiber* 0g
Sodium 805mg *Potassium* 145mg *Calcium* 77mg *Iron* 0.3mg
Magnesium 31mg *Copper* 0.2mg *Vitamin B*$_{12}$ 1.4mcg

Soy Nuts

A great nut choice for dieters, soy nuts are similar in texture and flavor to peanuts, but 50 percent lower in fat and 50 percent higher in protein. They are made from whole soybeans that have been soaked in water and baked until crisp and brown.

benefits

If you are not a fan of tofu and other soy products, soy nuts offer a tasty way to get the array of benefits found in soy. For dieters, soy nuts offer a lower-calorie way to enjoy the flavor and crunch of eating nuts and provide an abundance of high-quality, complete protein for long-lasting energy, as well as fiber to help keep hunger at bay. They contain powerful isoflavones, a phytonutrient that may help prevent certain types of cancer, fight heart disease and improve bone density. Soy nuts are also loaded with blood pressure-lowering potassium.

selection and storage

Packaged soy nuts are available oil or dry roasted, salted or unsalted, flavored, and even covered in yogurt or chocolate. Store in a cool, dry place for up to six months. Once the package is opened, store in an airtight container.

preparation and serving tips

Soy nuts make a great snack alone or combined with fiber-packed cereals, dried fruit and other nuts. They can be used as a crunchy topping for salads. To make soy nuts at home, soak dry soybeans in water for 6 to 8 hours, then drain and spread them in a single layer on an oiled baking sheet. Roast at 350°F for 30 to 50 minutes, stirring often until well browned.

nutrients per serving:

Soy Nuts, dry roasted without salt
1 ounce

Calories 132
Protein 10g
Total Fat 7g
Saturated Fat 1g
Cholesterol 0mg
Carbohydrate 9g
Dietary Fiber 5g
Sodium 0mg
Potassium 410mg
Calcium 39mg
Iron 1.1mg
Folate 59mcg
Magnesium 41mg
Vitamin E <1mg

Spaghetti Squash

Spaghetti squash is a magical food for dieters; it starts as a hard yellow squash and ends as a heaping bowl of pasta (and an extra serving of veggies)!

benefits

By substituting spaghetti squash for whole wheat spaghetti, you'll save 75 percent of the calories you would have consumed. (Spaghetti squash has 42 calories per cup while whole wheat spaghetti has 174.) It is also a decent source of fiber and offers a fair amount of vitamins A and C, potassium and iron.

selection and storage

Spaghetti squash is available year-round with a peak season from early fall through winter. It is oblong and usually bright yellow in color. Choose squash that is hard and smooth; avoid greenish squash, which may not be ripe, and those with bruises or signs of damage. Store spaghetti squash at room temperature for several weeks.

preparation and serving tips

Cut the squash lengthwise and remove the seeds; microwave whole squash 3 minutes to soften it for easier cutting. Cook until the flesh is tender and strands of squash are easily separated—about 8 to 10 minutes in the microwave or 45 minutes to 1 hour in a 350°F oven. After cooking, remove and separate the spaghetti-like strands from the shell with a fork and serve with desired sauces and toppings.

nutrients per serving:

Spaghetti Squash
½ cup cooked

Calories 21 *Protein* 1g *Total Fat* 0g *Saturated Fat* 0g
Cholesterol 0mg *Carbohydrate* 5g *Dietary Fiber* 1g
Sodium 15mg *Potassium* 90mg *Calcium* 16mg *Iron* 0.3mg
Vitamin A 85 IU *Vitamin C* 3mg *Folate* 6mcg

nutrients per serving:

Calories 240
Calories from Fat 25%
Protein 10g

Carbohydrate 41g
Fiber 6g
Total Fat 6g

Saturated Fat 3g
Cholesterol 15mg
Sodium 440mg

southwest spaghetti squash

- 1 spaghetti squash (about 3 pounds)
- 1 can (about 14 ounces) Mexican-style diced tomatoes
- 1 can (about 14 ounces) low-sodium black beans, rinsed and drained
- ½ cup (2 ounces) shredded Monterey Jack cheese, divided
- ¼ cup finely chopped fresh cilantro
- 1 teaspoon ground cumin
- ¼ teaspoon garlic salt
- ¼ teaspoon black pepper

1. Preheat oven to 350°F. Spray baking sheet and 1½-quart baking dish with nonstick cooking spray.

2. Cut squash in half lengthwise. Remove and discard seeds. Place squash, cut side down, on prepared baking sheet. Bake 45 minutes or just until tender.

3. Shred hot squash with fork; place in large bowl. (Use oven mitts to protect hands.) Add tomatoes, beans, ¼ cup cheese, cilantro, cumin, garlic salt and pepper; toss well.

4. Spoon mixture into prepared baking dish. Sprinkle with remaining ¼ cup cheese. Bake 30 to 35 minutes or until heated through.   *Makes 4 servings*

Spinach

Spinach is a nutritional superstar among greens; it's packed with fiber, iron and vitamins A and C.

nutrients per serving:

**Spinach
1 cup raw**

Calories 7
Protein 1g
Total Fat 0g
Saturated Fat 0g
Cholesterol 0mg
Carbohydrate 1g
Dietary Fiber 1g
Sodium 25mg
Potassium 165mg
Calcium 30mg
Iron 0.9mg
Vitamin A 2,813 IU
Vitamin C 8mg
Folate 58mcg

benefits

Spinach is loaded with vitamins and minerals and has twice as much fiber as most other cooking or salad greens. Like other dark greens, spinach is an excellent source of beta-carotene, a powerful disease-fighting antioxidant that's been shown to reduce the risk of developing cataracts as well as fight heart disease and cancer. Spinach is great for you, both raw and cooked, but cooking spinach concentrates its nutrients and fiber, giving you more per serving.

selection and storage

Choose spinach with crisp, dark green leaves; avoid limp or yellowing leaves. Refrigerate unwashed spinach in a loose plastic bag for three to four days. Prewashed bags of fresh spinach are readily available. Frozen and canned spinach are also convenient options.

preparation and serving tips

Raw spinach makes a wonderful salad either on its own or mixed with other leafy greens. Chopped raw spinach can be added to many cooked dishes such as soups, sauces, casseroles and chilis. To serve cooked spinach as a side, simmer the leaves in a small amount of water for about 5 minutes or until the leaves just begin to wilt. Top with lemon juice, seasoned vinegar and sautéed garlic.

light greek spanakopita

Olive oil cooking spray
1 teaspoon olive oil
1 large onion, quartered and sliced
2 cloves garlic, minced
1 package (10 ounces) frozen chopped spinach, thawed and squeezed dry
½ cup reduced-fat feta cheese crumbles
5 sheets phyllo dough, thawed*
½ cup cholesterol-free egg substitute
¼ teaspoon nutmeg
¼ to ½ teaspoon black pepper
⅛ teaspoon salt

*Thaw entire package of phyllo dough overnight in refrigerator.

1. Preheat oven to 375°F. Spray 8-inch square baking pan with cooking spray.

2. Heat oil in large skillet over medium heat. Add onion; cook and stir 7 to 8 minutes or until translucent. Add garlic; cook and stir 30 seconds. Add spinach and feta cheese; cook and stir until spinach is heated through. Remove from heat.

3. Place one sheet of phyllo dough on counter with long side toward you. (Cover remaining sheets with damp towel until needed.) Spray right half of phyllo with cooking spray; fold left half over sprayed half. Place sheet in prepared pan. (Two edges will hang over sides of pan.) Spray top of sheet. Spray and fold two more sheets of phyllo the same way. Place sheets in pan perpendicular so edges will hang over all four sides of pan. Spray each sheet after it is placed in pan.

4. Combine egg substitute, nutmeg, pepper and salt in small bowl. Stir into spinach mixture. Spread over phyllo in pan.

5. Spray and fold one sheet of phyllo as above; place on top of filling, tucking ends under filling. Bring all overhanging edges of phyllo over top sheet; spray lightly. Spray and fold last sheet; place over top sheet, tucking ends under. Spray lightly.

6. Bake 25 to 27 minutes or until top is barely browned. Cool 10 to 15 minutes before serving.   *Makes 4 servings*

nutrients per serving:

Calories 172	**Total Fat** 6g
Calories from Fat 31%	**Saturated Fat** 2g
Protein 10g	**Cholesterol** 5mg
Carbohydrate 18g	**Sodium** 580mg
Fiber 3g	

Strawberries

Sweet, juicy strawberries make a great breakfast, snack or dessert for dieters. As a bonus, they are low in calories and high in fiber and nutrients.

benefits

At a mere 49 calories per cup, strawberries are a sweet, low-calorie, fiber-filled substitute for high-calorie desserts and snacks. They are a super source of vitamin C—better even than oranges—and their seeds are loaded with insoluble fiber. Strawberries are one of the top 20 fruits in antioxidant capacity. They contain ellagic acid, which has anticancer, antiviral and antibacterial properties. Recent research suggests that strawberries may be able to reduce inflammation and boost metabolism as well as help control blood sugar. They are also loaded with potassium.

selection and storage

Look for plump strawberries that are ruby red and evenly colored with green, leafy tops. Avoid those that appear mushy or bruised. Bigger does not equal better; in fact, smaller berries tend to be the sweetest. Avoid strawberries in containers with juice stains or berries packed tightly with plastic wrap. Strawberries spoil quickly so eat them within a day or two of purchasing.

preparation and serving tips

Strawberries are delicious on their own, especially topped with a little balsamic vinegar to bring out their natural sweetness. Add sliced strawberries to cereal, oatmeal, spinach salads, yogurt and gelatin molds. Try blending overripe strawberries into smoothies, orange juice or lemonade.

nutrients per serving:

**Strawberries
1 cup halves**

Calories 49
Protein 1g
Total Fat 0g
Saturated Fat 0g
Cholesterol 0mg
Carbohydrate 12g
Dietary Fiber 3g
Sodium 0mg
Potassium 235mg
Calcium 24mg
Iron 0.6mg
Vitamin A 18 IU
Vitamin C 89mg
Folate 36mcg

nutrients per serving:

Calories 89
Calories from Fat 66%
Protein 3g
Carbohydrate 8g
Fiber 1g

Total Fat 5g
Saturated Fat 3g
Cholesterol 10mg
Sodium 138mg

strawberry mousse

1 package (4-serving size)
     strawberry sugar-free gelatin
½ cup boiling water
2 cups fresh sliced strawberrles,
     divided
½ cup reduced-fat cream cheese
½ cup cold water
¼ teaspoon almond extract
1 cup reduced-fat whipped topping,
     plus additional for garnish
     (optional)

1. Place gelatin in small bowl. Pour boiling water over gelatin; stir until completely dissolved. Pour gelatin mixture into blender. Add 1 cup sliced strawberries, cream cheese, cold water and almond extract; blend 1 minute or until smooth.

2. Pour mixture into medium bowl. Thoroughly whisk whipped topping into mixture (make sure gelatin mix does not settle to bottom).

3. Pour mousse into six serving cups. Refrigerate at least 2 hours or until set. Top mousse with remaining 1 cup sliced strawberries and dollop of whipped topping, if desired.   *Makes 6 servings*

Sweet Potatoes

Sweet potatoes are most famous for their role in the traditional Thanksgiving meal but they are versatile and delicious beyond the holiday table.

benefits

The natural sweet flavor of sweet potatoes doesn't need to be enhanced by any sauces or butter. And the richness goes beyond their great taste; they are loaded with potassium, vitamin C, and fiber. Their vibrant orange flesh indicates the presence of beta-carotene, which helps fight chronic diseases like cancer and heart disease as well as inflammatory diseases.

selection and storage

Sweet potatoes are commonly and mistakenly called yams but they are not the same. Look for sweet potatoes that are small to medium in size with smooth, unbruised skin. They are fragile and spoil easily so be careful as any cut or bruise on the surface will quickly spread, ruining the whole potato. Store potatoes at room temperature for about a week; do not refrigerate.

preparation and serving tips

Sweet potatoes can be prepared in several ways. Boil, bake or microwave whole unpeeled potatoes; leaving the peel intact prevents excessive loss of nutrients and locks in the natural sweetness. Try sweet potatoes mashed, roasted or cut into sticks and baked for sweet potato fries. Add them to quick breads and muffins for added moistness, flavor and nutrients.

nutrients per serving:

Sweet Potato
½ cup flesh, cooked

Calories 90 *Protein* 2g *Total Fat* 0g *Saturated Fat* 0g
Cholesterol 0mg *Carbohydrate* 21g *Dietary Fiber* 3.5g
Sodium 35mg *Potassium* 475mg *Calcium* 38mg *Iron* 0.7mg
Vitamin A 19,218 IU *Vitamin C* 20mg *Folate* 6mcg

sweet potato bisque

- **1 pound sweet potatoes, peeled and cut into 2-inch chunks**
- **2 teaspoons butter**
- **½ cup finely chopped onion**
- **1 teaspoon curry powder**
- **½ teaspoon ground coriander**
- **¼ teaspoon salt**
- **⅔ cup unsweetened apple juice**
- **1 cup buttermilk**
- **¼ cup water**
- **Fresh chopped chives (optional)**

1. Place potatoes in large saucepan; cover with water. Bring to a boil over high heat. Cook 15 minutes or until potatoes are fork-tender. Drain.

2. Meanwhile, melt butter in small saucepan over medium heat. Add onion; cook and stir 2 minutes. Add curry powder, coriander and salt; cook and stir 1 minute or until onion is tender. Remove from heat; stir in apple juice.

3. Combine potatoes, buttermilk and onion mixture in food processor or blender; process until smooth. Return to saucepan; stir in ¼ cup water, if necessary, to thin to desired consistency. Cook and stir over medium heat until heated through. *Do not boil.* Garnish with chives. *Makes 4 servings*

nutrients per serving:

Calories 160
Calories from Fat 15%
Protein 4g
Carbohydrate 31g
Fiber 4g
Total Fat 3g
Saturated Fat 1g
Cholesterol 2mg
Sodium 231mg

Tangerines

A type of mandarin orange, tangerines are intensely sweet and juicy and make a great portable low-calorie snack. If you want to go seedless, try the closely related clementine.

benefits

At only 47 calories per fruit, tangerines are wonderful sweet substitutes for high-calorie desserts and snacks. According to recent research, nobiletin, a flavonoid in tangerines, may help prevent obesity and offer protection against type 2 diabetes and atherosclerosis. While tangerines have only one third as much vitamin C and folate as oranges, they provide three times as much cancer-fighting vitamin A. They are also a decent source of potassium and soluble fiber.

selection and storage

These loose-skinned fruits are at their peak from November through June. Other varieties of mandarin oranges include the clementine, satsuma and honey tangerine (most canned mandarin oranges are satsumas). Choose fresh tangerines that feel heavy for their size with smooth unblemished skin. They should feel soft but not mushy. Store in the refrigerator for up to a week.

preparation and serving tips

Tangerines and other mandarins are great on their own but make a tangy addition to various dishes. Add seeded tangerine segments to spinach salads, fruit salads, coleslaws and tuna salads. Add fresh squeezed tangerine juice to dressings and marinades.

nutrients per serving:

**Tangerine
1 medium**

Calories 47
Protein 1g
Total Fat 0g
Saturated Fat 0g
Cholesterol 0mg
Carbohydrate 12g
Dietary Fiber 1.5g
Sodium 0mg
Potassium 145mg
Calcium 33mg
Iron 0.1mg
Vitamin A 599 IU
Vitamin C 24mg
Folate 14mcg

nutrients per serving:

Calories 45
Calories from Fat 0%
Protein 0g
Carbohydrate 11g
Fiber 0g

Total Fat 0g
Saturated Fat 0g
Cholesterol 0mg
Sodium 0mg

sparkling tangerine-cranberry green tea

**2 cups chilled unsweetened
    green tea**
**1 cup freshly squeezed tangerine
    juice (3 to 4 tangerines)**
½ cup cranberry juice
**1 cup seltzer water
    Ice cubes
    Tangerine slices (optional)
    Cranberries (optional)**

1. Mix tea, tangerine juice and cranberry juice in large pitcher. Stir in seltzer.

2. Serve over ice in four glasses. Garnish with tangerine slices and cranberries.   *Makes 4 servings*

Tofu

Tofu may be a stranger to nonvegetarians but it shouldn't be. It has a creamy flavor on its own that pairs well with everything and absorbs the flavors of seasonings and sauces.

benefits

Tofu is the perfect way to get protein into your diet without the fat and calories. It is a nutritionally complete protein like chicken breasts. Tofu contains beneficial amounts of iron like meat products, but it has no cholesterol. It also contains soy isoflavones and other phytonutrients that are linked with reduced risks of heart disease and some cancers. Also, depending on how it is processed, tofu can be a terrific source of calcium.

selection and storage

Tofu is made by curdling the whey that is extracted from ground cooked soybeans, similar to the cheese making process.

It is available both silken and as blocks in soft, firm or extra-firm textures. Tofu can be found refrigerated in individual packages or in shelf-stable aseptically sealed containers. Once opened, tofu should be covered in water that is changed daily and stored in the refrigerator for up to a week. Tofu can be frozen for up to five months but the texture will change.

preparation and serving tips

Tofu is versatile and can be used in the same way as meat. Try adding cubed tofu to stir-fries, soups, stews, chilis, casseroles and even pasta dishes near the end of the cooking time. Silken tofu can be used in salad dressings, sauces and even as a replacement for eggs in baked goods.

nutrients per serving:

Tofu, regular ½ cup raw

Calories 94
Protein 10g
Total Fat 6g
Saturated Fat 1g
Cholesterol 0mg
Carbohydrate 2g
Dietary Fiber 0.5g
Sodium 10mg
Potassium 150mg
Calcium 434mg
Iron 6.7mg
Vitamin A 105 IU
Vitamin C 0mg
Folate 19mcg

tofu, vegetable and curry stir-fry

- 1 package (about 14 ounces) extra-firm reduced-fat tofu, cut into ¾-inch cubes
- ¾ cup reduced-fat coconut milk
- 2 tablespoons fresh lime juice
- 1 tablespoon curry powder
- 2 teaspoons dark sesame oil, divided
- 4 cups broccoli florets (1½-inch pieces)
- 2 medium red bell peppers, cut into short, thin strips
- 1 medium red onion, cut into thin wedges
- ¼ teaspoon salt

1. Press tofu cubes between layers of paper towels to remove excess moisture. Combine coconut milk, lime juice and curry powder in medium bowl; set aside.

2. Heat 1 teaspoon oil in large nonstick skillet over medium heat. Add tofu; cook 10 minutes or until lightly browned on all sides, turning cubes often. Remove to plate.

3. Add remaining 1 teaspoon oil to same skillet; increase heat to high. Add broccoli, bell pepper and onion; cook and stir about 5 minutes or until vegetables are crisp-tender. Add tofu and coconut milk mixture; bring to a boil, stirring constantly. Season with salt.

Makes 4 servings

nutrients per serving:

Calories 167
Calories from Fat 42%
Protein 12g
Carbohydrate 16g
Fiber 5g

Total Fat 8g
Saturated Fat 2g
Cholesterol 0mg
Sodium 159mg

Tomatoes

Although technically a fruit, tomatoes are one of the most popular vegetables in America. Regardless of how you categorize them, tomatoes are low in calories, rich in nutrients and a natural part of any weight-loss program.

benefits

Tomatoes are rich in lycopene, a cancer-fighting antioxidant that gives the tomato its red color. They are one of the most significant dietary sources of vitamin C and contain beta-carotene and several other carotenoids that may help prevent heart disease and cancer. In addition, tomatoes are an important source of potassium, a mineral that is critical to heart, muscle and nerve functions.

selection and storage

There are many varieties of tomatoes, ranging in color from classic red to yellow, green and purple. They also vary in size: cherry, grape, plum and the large beefsteak. Tomatoes are available year-round but vine-ripened tomatoes, available in summer months, have the best flavor. Look for tomatoes that are firm and well shaped with a noticeable fragrance. They should be heavy for their size and yield to slight pressure. Do not store them in the refrigerator as cold temperatures ruin their taste and texture. Canned tomatoes are available in several varieties and flavors.

preparation and serving tips

Tomatoes are delicious raw in salads, on sandwiches or on their own with a sprinkling of sea salt and freshly ground pepper. They're also a great addition to a variety of cooked dishes like stews, chilis and pasta sauces.

nutrients per serving:

**Tomatoes, red
1 medium**

Calories 22
Protein 1g
Total Fat 0g
Saturated Fat 0g
Cholesterol 0mg
Carbohydrate 5g
Dietary Fiber 1.5g
Sodium 5mg
Potassium 290mg
Calcium 12mg
Iron 0.3mg
Vitamin A 1,025 IU
Vitamin C 17mg
Folate 18mcg

quinoa-stuffed tomatoes

½ cup uncooked quinoa
1 cup water
½ teaspoon salt, divided
1 tablespoon olive oil
1 red bell pepper, chopped
⅓ cup chopped green onion
⅛ teaspoon black pepper
⅛ teaspoon dried thyme
1 tablespoon butter
8 plum tomatoes,* halved lengthwise, seeded, hollowed out

*Or substitute 4 medium tomatoes.

1. Preheat oven to 325°F. Place quinoa in fine-mesh strainer; rinse well. Bring water and ¼ teaspoon salt to a boil in small saucepan. Stir in quinoa. Reduce heat to low; cover and simmer 12 to 14 minutes or until quinoa is tender and water is absorbed.

nutrients per serving:

Calories 95	**Total Fat** 4g
Calories from Fat 32%	**Saturated Fat** 1g
Protein 6g	**Cholesterol** 4mg
Carbohydrate 13g	**Sodium** 165mg
Fiber 3g	

2. Heat oil in large skillet over medium-high heat. Add bell pepper; cook and stir 7 to 10 minutes or until tender. Stir in quinoa, green onions, remaining ¼ teaspoon salt, black pepper and thyme. Add butter; cook and stir until melted. Remove from heat.

3. Arrange tomato halves in 8-inch square baking dish. Fill with quinoa mixture. Bake 15 to 20 minutes or until tomatoes are tender.

Makes 8 servings

167

Tuna

Tuna is naturally lean and high in protein—a winning combination when you're watching your weight.

benefits

Protein, which is important for building and maintaining muscle, often comes accompanied by saturated fat and lots of calories. Tuna, however, is one of the best sources of lean protein. Water-packed canned or fresh tuna is also a great source of omega-3 fatty acids, unsaturated fats that have been shown to have numerous significant health benefits: they help reduce inflammation throughout the body, lower triglycerides, promote heart health and reduce heart arrhythmias as well as help treat some forms of depression. Experts recommend eating fish that provides omega-3s twice a week. Tuna also provides potassium, selenium and vitamin B12.

selection and storage

Canned tuna is available packed in water or oil. Common varieties of tuna include yellowfin, which is deep red in color and sold canned as light tuna, and albacore, which is white to pale pink and labeled "white" tuna on cans. Fresh tuna is available as steaks, fillets or pieces and should be used within a day or two or frozen, tightly wrapped, for up to a month.

preparation and serving tips

Lighten up your tuna salad by going easy on the mayonnaise and adding fresh lemon juice, nonfat Greek yogurt and mustard. To add bulk, flavor and nutrients, try mixing in chopped celery, fennel, bell peppers, carrots, water chestnuts, jicama, parsley, fruit or nuts. Fresh tuna steaks can be marinated and grilled or broiled.

nutrients per serving:

Tuna, canned in water
3 ounces

Calories 109 **Protein** 20g **Total Fat** 2.5g **Saturated Fat** 0.5g
Cholesterol 36mg **Carbohydrate** 0g **Dietary Fiber** 0g
Sodium 40mg **Potassium** 200mg **Calcium** 12mg **Iron** 0.8mg
Selenium 56mcg **Phosphorus** 184mg **Vitamin B12** 1mcg

pasta and tuna filled peppers

- ¾ cup uncooked ditalini pasta
- 4 large green bell peppers
- 1 cup chopped seeded fresh tomatoes
- 1 can (about 6 ounces) white tuna packed in water, drained and flaked
- ½ cup chopped celery
- ½ cup (2 ounces) shredded reduced-fat Cheddar cheese
- ¼ cup fat-free mayonnaise or salad dressing
- 1 teaspoon salt-free garlic and herb seasoning
- 2 tablespoons shredded reduced-fat Cheddar cheese (optional)

1. Cook pasta according to package directions. Drain; set aside.

2. Cut thin slice from top of each bell pepper; remove seeds and membranes. Rinse bell peppers; place, cut side down, on paper towels to drain.*

3. Combine pasta, tomatoes, tuna, celery, ½ cup cheese, mayonnaise and seasoning in large bowl; mix well. Spoon evenly into bell peppers.

4. Place on large microwavable plate; cover with waxed paper. Microwave on HIGH 7 to 8 minutes, turning halfway through cooking time. Top evenly with 2 tablespoons cheese before serving, if desired.   *Makes 4 servings*

For more tender bell peppers, cook in boiling water 2 minutes. Plunge into cold water; drain upside down on paper towels before filling.

nutrients per serving:

Calories 216	**Carbohydrate** 27g
Calories from Fat 16%	**Fiber** 2g
Protein 19g	**Total Fat** 4g
	Saturated Fat 1g
	Cholesterol 26mg
	Sodium 574mg

Turkey Breast

Turkey breast meat is even lower in fat than chicken breast, so feel free to change up your poultry routine and swap turkey for chicken in your favorite dishes.

benefits

Skinless turkey breast is one of the leanest meats, making it a great way to get satisfying protein with very little saturated fat. It is rich in selenium, a mineral with anticancer properties that also plays a role in thyroid function, and zinc, a mineral that helps maintain a healthy immune system. Turkey contains vitamins B_6 and B_{12}, which are essential for energy production.

selection and storage

There's no need to buy a whole turkey—look for turkey breasts in the meat department. Purchase it with the skin, which is less expensive than skinless. Prepare it with the skin on to lock in the juices; just be sure to remove the skin before you serve it. Ground turkey breast is available but be sure to check the label; some ground turkey products also include dark meat, which is higher in calories and fat. Turkey breast luncheon meat is lean and convenient. Store wrapped fresh turkey in the coldest part of your refrigerator and use within two to three days. Turkey breast can also be frozen.

preparation and serving tips

To keep lean turkey breast moist, cook it with the skin and remove it before eating. Grill or roast turkey breast to an internal temperature of 165°F. Ground turkey is a great substitute for ground beef and works well in burgers, chilis and meat loaves.

nutrients per serving:

Turkey breast, skinless 3 ounces roasted

Calories 115
Protein 26g
Total Fat 0.6g
Saturated Fat 0.2g
Cholesterol 71mg
Carbohydrate 0g
Dietary Fiber 0g
Sodium 44mg
Potassium 248mg
Zinc 1.5mg
Iron 1.3mg
Vitamin B_6 0.5mg
Vitamin B_{12} 0.3mcg
Selenium 27mcg

170

Turnips

For a change of pace from potatoes, try turnips. They can be prepared in many of the same ways as potatoes, and have about two-thirds fewer calories.

benefits

A cup of turnips has about 30 calories and enough soluble fiber to make you feel satisfied. Turnips provide a decent amount of vitamin C, an antioxidant that protects the heart and immune system, as well as potassium and calcium. Turnip greens are low in calories and provide beta-carotene and more vitamin C than the turnip root itself.

selection and storage

Turnips are available year-round, but the best ones are available in the fall. Baby turnips are the most tender and sweet and can be eaten whole, including their leaves. Turnips come in yellow, orange, white and red varieties. Look for turnips with smooth unblemished skins. Store in the crisper drawer of the refrigerator and use within a week.

preparation and serving tips

To prepare turnips, first remove the leaf and root ends. Peel larger turnips, but smaller turnips can be cooked without peeling. They can be boiled, baked, braised or steamed and mashed as a side dish or added to stews, soups or vegetable dishes. Baby turnips can be eaten raw. Raw turnips greens have a pungent flavor that mellows after cooking; sauté them with olive oil and garlic for a savory side dish.

nutrients per serving:

Turnips
½ cup cooked

Calories 17 **Protein** 1g **Total Fat** 0g **Saturated Fat** 0g
Cholesterol 0mg **Carbohydrate** 4g **Dietary Fiber** 1.5g
Sodium 10mg **Potassium** 140mg **Calcium** 26mg **Iron** 0.1mg
Vitamin C 9mg **Folate** 7mcg

Water Chestnuts

Water chestnuts resemble chestnuts, although they are not a nut. This crunchy tuberous vegetable actually comes from an aquatic plant.

benefits

Water chestnuts are most commonly used in Asian cuisines but they add a hint of sweetness, fiber and protein to any dish for very few calories. They are very low in sodium and a good source of potassium and magnesium, so they help keep blood pressure low. Although fresh water chestnuts are nutritionally superior, canned options are suitable substitutes.

selection and storage

Water chestnuts are available fresh in most Asian markets. Choose those that are firm with no signs of shriveling. They should be stored tightly wrapped in the refrigerator and used within a week. Peel off their brownish-black skin before using. Canned water chestnuts are readily available either sliced or whole. Be sure to rinse canned varieties before cooking to get rid of any excess sodium.

preparation and serving tips

Water chestnuts are most often used in stir-fries and other Asian dishes, but they can be incorporated into a variety of other foods. Add them to salads for an extra crunch, or chop them and add to tuna salads, chicken salads or veggie dips. Try them cooked with vegetables, such as asparagus or green beans. For a fun appetizer, wrap whole water chestnuts with turkey bacon and broil or grill them.

nutrients per serving:

Water Chestnuts
½ cup raw

Calories 60 **Protein** 1g
Total Fat 0g **Saturated Fat** 0g
Cholesterol 0mg **Carbohydrate** 15g
Dietary Fiber 2g **Sodium** 9mg
Potassium 362mg **Calcium** 7mg
Phosphorus 39mg **Magnesium** 14mg
Vitamin C 3mg **Folate** 10mcg

honey-mustard chicken salad

4 ounces canned low-sodium white
   chicken, rinsed and drained
½ cup sliced seedless red grapes
¼ cup chopped water chestnuts
2 tablespoons fat-free low-sodium
   honey-mustard salad dressing
¼ teaspoon grated lemon peel
1 cup fresh spinach, stemmed
1 teaspoon pine nuts, toasted*
⅛ teaspoon black pepper

*To toast pine nuts, spread in single layer in small
skillet. Cook over medium heat 1 to 2 minutes, stirring
frequently, until nuts are lightly browned. Remove from
skillet immediately. Cool before using.

1. Combine chicken, grapes, water chestnuts,
salad dressing and lemon peel in small bowl;
toss to coat. Let stand 5 minutes.

2. Arrange spinach on plate; top with salad and
sprinkle with pine nuts. Season with pepper.

Makes 1 serving

nutrients per serving:

Calories 213
Calories from Fat 14%
Protein 17g
Carbohydrate 33g
Fiber 2g
Total Fat 4g
Saturated Fat <1g
Cholesterol 27mg
Sodium 603mg

Watercress

A member of the cruciferous vegetable family, watercress is among the more nutritious salad greens. This delicate leafy green has a surprisingly robust peppery flavor.

benefits

Watercress is very low in calories and loaded with the antioxidants lutein, beta-carotene and vitamin C, which help protect the eyes and combat free radicals that can lead to heart disease and cancer cell growth. Vitamin C also boosts the immune system and helps keep the gums healthy. Watercress contains more calcium than spinach and this mineral works together with potassium to help normalize blood pressure. The phytonutrients in watercress have been shown to help protect against lung cancer.

selection and storage

Watercress is available year-round, usually sold in small bunches. Look for crisp leaves with deep, vibrant color free of yellowing or wilting. Store it in the refrigerator for up to five days.

preparation and serving tips

Rinse watercress well and dry the leaves right before using. Use it in salads, sandwiches, soups and a variety of cooked dishes. The pungent taste of watercress is complemented by citrus flavors, so try serving it with lemon juice or citrus-based salad dressings and sauces. Or toss it with orange or grapefruit slices for a refreshing and flavorful fruit salad. When using watercress in cooked dishes, add it at the end of cooking and serve immediately.

nutrients per serving:

**Watercress
1 cup raw**

Calories 4
Protein 1g
Total Fat 0g
Saturated Fat 0g
Cholesterol 0mg
Carbohydrate <1g
Dietary Fiber <1g
Sodium 15mg
Potassium 110mg
Calcium 41mg
Iron 0.1mg
Vitamin A 1,085 IU
Vitamin C 15mg
Folate 3mcg

Watermelon

For a refreshing alternative to sugary treats, try watermelon. Everyone's favorite summer fruit is sweet and juicy and loaded with fiber and nutrients.

benefits

Watermelon is considered a perfect diet food—it is 92 percent water and high in fiber. Watermelon's bright red flesh is a valuable source of lycopene, a phytonutrient that has been shown to reduce the risks of prostate, breast and colon cancers. And it is abundant in vitamin C and beta-carotene, disease-fighting antioxidants that help prevent heart disease, cancer and other chronic conditions. Watermelon is also a good source of potassium, which helps keep blood pressure down and may also reduce the risk of developing kidney stones and prevent age-related bone loss.

selection and storage

Look for watermelon, with or without seeds, that is evenly shaped with no bruises, cracks or soft spots. Select one that is heavy for its size and sounds hollow when tapped. Watermelon doesn't ripen much after it is picked. Look for signs of ripeness, including a firm underside with a yellowish color; if it is white or green, the melon is not yet mature.

A whole watermelon keeps in the refrigerator up to a week, but cut watermelon should be eaten as soon as possible.

preparation and serving tips

Rinse watermelon well before cutting. The flesh can be cubed, sliced or scooped into balls. Watermelon tastes best when served icy cold. Try a cold melon soup, or toss cubed watermelon in a salad with a salty cheese like feta. A hollowed out watermelon makes a great serving dish for fruit salad.

Wheat Berries

Wheat berries are whole unprocessed kernels of wheat that can be prepared and served just like rice. Cooked wheat berries have a chewy bite and a subtle nutty, earthy flavor.

benefits

Wheat berries are the quintessential whole wheat; only the inedible outer layer is removed, leaving the berries nutritionally intact and filled with fiber. This whole grain is also a good source of satisfying protein that provides a long-lasting source of energy. Wheat berries are a good source of magnesium, which along with potassium can help to lower blood pressure and may also prevent the development of type 2 diabetes. They also contain a decent amount of niacin, a B vitamin that helps convert food into energy, as well as selenium, an antioxidant mineral that helps regulate thyroid activity.

selection and storage

Wheat berries are often available in bulk bins in the natural foods or grain section of the supermarket. They are usually labeled either "spring wheat" or "winter wheat" based on the time of year the wheat is sown. Most wheat berries are considered hard wheat, which is higher in protein. Hard wheat berries may be ground into whole wheat flour. Store uncooked wheat berries in a cool, dry place.

preparation and serving tips

Before cooking, rinse wheat berries under cool water. Add them to boiling water and simmer for about 1 hour; they will double in size. Add cooked wheat berries to soups, salads or sautéed vegetables, or try them in a holiday stuffing.

nutrients per serving:

Wheat Berries
½ cup cooked

Calories 158
Protein 7g
Total Fat 0.5g
Saturated Fat 0g
Cholesterol 0mg
Carbohydrate 33g
Dietary Fiber 6g
Sodium 0mg
Potassium 163mg
Calcium 12mg
Iron 1.7mg
Magnesium 60mg
Selenium 34mcg
Niacin 2.7mg

wheat berry apple salad

1 cup uncooked wheat berries
(whole wheat kernels)
½ teaspoon salt
2 apples (1 red and 1 green),
unpeeled, chopped
½ cup dried cranberries
⅓ cup chopped walnuts
1 stalk celery, chopped
Grated peel and juice of 1 medium
orange
2 tablespoons rice wine vinegar
1½ tablespoons chopped fresh mint
Lettuce leaves (optional)

1. Place wheat berries and salt in large saucepan; cover with 1 inch of water. Bring to a boil. Reduce heat to low. Cover and cook 45 minutes to 1 hour or until wheat berries are tender but chewy, stirring occasionally, adding additional water if needed. Drain and let cool.*

2. Combine wheat berries, apples, cranberries, walnuts, celery, orange peel, orange juice, vinegar and mint in large bowl. Cover and refrigerate at least 1 hour to allow flavors to blend. Serve on lettuce leaves, if desired.

Makes about 6 servings

To cut cooking time by 20 to 30 minutes, soak wheat berries in water overnight. Drain and cover with 1 inch fresh water before cooking. Wheat berries can also be made up to 4 days in advance and stored in the refrigerator.

nutrients per serving:

Calories 193
Calories from Fat 25%
Protein 6g
Carbohydrate 33g
Fiber 5g
Total Fat 6g
Saturated Fat <1g
Cholesterol 0mg
Sodium 210mg

Wheat Bran

Wheat bran, the outer layer of the wheat kernel, is bursting with fiber. Including more fiber-filled whole wheat foods in your diet will help your weight-loss efforts.

benefits

Wheat bran is a concentrated source of insoluble fiber, the type that helps you feel full and keeps your digestive tract healthy. It also takes longer to chew and eat than refined wheat, giving your brain time to register that your stomach is full. Wheat bran is a good source of B vitamins, including niacin and vitamin B_6, that help convert food into energy. It also provides an array of important minerals, including iron, zinc, potassium and magnesium. If you aren't used to a lot of fiber in your diet, add high fiber foods like wheat bran gradually, and be sure to drink plenty of liquids.

selection and storage

Wheat bran is usually available in the bulk bins in the natural foods section of the supermarket or it may be found with grains or cereal. Store wheat bran in an airtight container in the refrigerator.

preparation and serving tips

Wheat bran can be added to many foods to boost fiber content. Sprinkle it over hot or cold cereals or on yogurt or applesauce. Add wheat bran to recipes for breads, cookies, muffins and pancakes. It can easily be added to ground meat dishes such as meat loaves or casseroles. Toasting wheat bran gives it an especially nutty flavor and crunchy texture.

nutrients per serving:

Wheat Bran
½ cup

Calories 63 **Protein** 5g **Total Fat** 1g **Saturated Fat** 0g
Cholesterol 0mg **Carbohydrate** 19g **Dietary Fiber** 12g
Sodium 0mg **Potassium** 345mg **Magnesium** 177mg
Iron 3.1mg **Zinc** 2.1mg **Niacin** 3.9mg **Vitamin B₆** 0.4mg

strawberry and peach crisp

1 cup frozen unsweetened peach slices,
   thawed and cut into 1-inch pieces
1 cup sliced fresh strawberries
3 teaspoons sugar, divided
¼ cup bran cereal flakes
2 tablespoons old-fashioned oats
1 tablespoon all-purpose flour
⅛ teaspoon ground cinnamon
⅛ teaspoon salt
2 teaspoons unsalted margarine, cut
   into small pieces

1. Preheat oven to 325°F. Spray 1½-quart glass baking dish with nonstick cooking spray.

2. Combine peaches and strawberries in baking dish. Sprinkle with 1 teaspoon sugar.

3. Combine remaining 2 teaspoons sugar, cereal, oats, flour, cinnamon and salt in small bowl. Cut in margarine with pastry blender or two knives until mixture resembles coarse crumbs. Sprinkle evenly over fruit.

4. Bake 20 minutes or until fruit is hot and topping is slightly browned.   *Makes 4 servings*

nutrients per serving:

Calories 80
Calories from Fat 24%
Protein 1g
Carbohydrate 15g
Fiber 3g
Total Fat 2g
Saturated Fat <1g
Cholesterol 0mg
Sodium 83mg

Wild Rice

Despite its name, wild rice is actually a long grain grass that was first discovered growing wild in marshy areas. It has a nutty flavor and chewy texture, and is lower in calories and higher in protein than regular rice.

nutrients per serving:

Wild Rice
½ cup cooked

Calories 83
Protein 3g
Total Fat 0g
Saturated Fat 0g
Cholesterol 0mg
Carbohydrate 18g
Dietary Fiber 1.5g
Sodium 0mg
Potassium 85mg
Calcium 2mg
Iron 0.5mg
Manganese 0.3mg
Vitamin A 2 IU
Folate 21mcg

benefits

Adding wild rice to your diet will add a ton of variety to your meals as well as fiber and nutrients. It actually has fewer calories than brown rice and provides the same amount of protein, so it will help you manage your appetite. Wild rice offers twice as much potassium as brown rice, too. It's rich in manganese, a mineral that's important for healthy thyroid function, which is essential in maintaining a healthy weight. Wild rice is also a good source of folate, a B vitamin that helps reduce the risk of heart disease.

selection and storage

Wild rice is available in most grocery stores. It is dark brown to black in color and is longer and thinner than long grain rice. It can be stored in a cool, dry place for a long time. Refrigerate leftover cooked wild rice up to one week or freeze it for later use.

preparation and serving tips

Clean wild rice before using. Place it in a bowl of cold water and stir it a few times. Let it stand for a minute (any debris will float to the top) and then pour off the water. Bring three parts water to a boil; add one part wild rice and simmer for 30 to 45 minutes. Wild rice can be served as a healthy side dish, added to soups or served cold as part of a vegetable and rice salad.

wild rice, cranberry and apple stuffing

- 4 medium acorn squash (about 2¼ pounds)
- 1 cup water
- 1 tablespoon olive oil or butter
- 1 medium apple, diced (about 1 cup)
- 2 stalks celery, diced (about ⅔ cup)
- 1 clove garlic, minced
- Pinch of dried or fresh thyme
- Pinch of dried sage
- 1 cup hot cooked white or brown rice
- 1 cup hot cooked wild rice
- ½ cup orange juice
- ¼ cup dried cranberries
- ¼ cup sliced green onions
- Salt and black pepper (optional)

1. Preheat oven to 400°F. Cut squash into halves. Scoop out and discard seeds.

2. Place squash, cut side down, in 13×9-inch baking dish. Add water to baking dish; bake 35 to 45 minutes or until fork-tender. Turn squash cut side up.

3. Heat oil in large saucepan over medium-high heat. Add apple, celery and garlic; cook and stir 5 minutes or until softened. Reduce heat to medium-low. Add thyme and sage; cook and stir 1 minute. Add white and wild rice, orange juice and cranberries; cook 1 minute or until heated through. Stir in green onions; season with salt and pepper.

4. Fill squash halves with stuffing.

Makes 8 servings

Yellow Squash

A type of summer squash, the yellow squash comes in both crookneck and straightneck varieties. They differ only in shape; nutritionally they are equally smart choices for your weight-loss plan.

benefits

Summer squash is even lower in calories than winter squash. Yellow squash is an excellent source of the antioxidants vitamin C and beta-carotene, which help to fight the inflammation that leads to heart disease and certain types of cancer. It's also a very good source of folate, which plays a role in heart health.

selection and storage

Yellow squash is at its peak during summer months but is available year-round. It should feel heavy for its size and have shiny, unblemished rinds. Look for summer squash that is small to average in size; larger squash may have harder rinds and tend to have larger seeds and stringy flesh. Yellow squash is very perishable and should be stored unwashed in a plastic bag in the refrigerator for up to five days.

preparation and serving tips

Wash yellow squash under cool running water and then cut off both ends. It can be sliced into rounds and enjoyed raw with dip or sliced or grated into thin strips and added to a fresh salad. Sauté with onions, bell peppers, eggplant and tomatoes for ratatouille or add it to almost any cooked dish for a touch of color and flavor.

nutrients per serving:

Yellow Squash
½ cup cooked

Calories 21 **Protein** 1g **Total Fat** 0g **Saturated Fat** 0g
Cholesterol 0mg **Carbohydrate** 3g **Dietary Fiber** 1g
Sodium 0mg **Potassium** 160mg **Calcium** 20mg **Iron** 0.3mg
Vitamin A 1,005 IU **Vitamin C** 10mg **Folate** 21mcg

vegetable napoleon

1 teaspoon salt-free garlic and
    herb seasoning
¼ teaspoon black pepper
¼ teaspoon garlic powder
1 large yellow summer squash, thinly
    sliced lengthwise
1 large zucchini, thinly sliced lengthwise
¼ cup (1 ounce) shredded reduced-fat
    mozzarella cheese
1 large tomato, thinly sliced*

For easier slicing, use a serrated bread knife.

1. Preheat oven to 350°F. Spray mini loaf pan with cooking spray. Combine seasoning, pepper and garlic powder in small bowl.

2. Layer one third of squash and zucchini in loaf pan. Sprinkle with one third of seasoning mixture and 1 tablespoon cheese. Top with tomato slices. Sprinkle with one third of seasoning mixture and 1 tablespoon of cheese. Top with remaining squash, seasoning mixture and cheese.

3. Bake 35 minutes or until vegetables are tender and cheese is melted. Remove from oven. Cool slightly before slicing.

Makes 2 servings

nutrients per serving:

Calories 78
Calories from Fat 25%
Protein 6g
Carbohydrate 9g
Fiber 3g
Total Fat 2g
Saturated Fat 1g
Cholesterol 6mg
Sodium 105mg

Yogurt

Yogurt is a nutrient-rich source of protein that supplies long-lasting energy and can help you manage your weight.

benefits

Yogurt provides significant protein and as much bone-building calcium as milk but is digested more easily because it contains live active bacterial cultures. These active bacteria also improve your immune system, help lower LDL "bad" cholesterol levels and suppress the growth of harmful bacteria in the intestine.

selection and storage

To keep fat and calories low, look for low-fat or nonfat yogurt. The addition of fruit or sweeteners adds calories, so look for plain varieties and add your own fruit or flavorings. Check for a "sell-by" date on the carton; it will keep for up to ten days past that date.

preparation and serving tips

Yogurt makes a great portable meal or snack on its own, but has several other great uses. Top your morning bowl of cereal with yogurt instead of milk or use it as a base for fresh fruit and juice smoothies. Yogurt also works great as a substitute for high-fat ingredients like sour cream and mayonnaise in tuna salads, chicken salads, dips and salad dressings.

nutrients per serving:

Yogurt, plain low-fat 1 cup

Calories 154
Protein 13g
Total Fat 4g
Saturated Fat 2.5g
Cholesterol 15mg
Carbohydrate 17g
Dietary Fiber 0g
Sodium 170mg
Potassium 575mg
Calcium 448mg
Iron 0.2mg
Vitamin A 125 IU
Vitamin C 2mg
Folate 27mcg

banana & chocolate chip pops

1 small ripe banana, sliced
1 cup nonfat banana yogurt
⅛ teaspoon ground nutmeg
2 tablespoons mini chocolate chips

1. Combine banana, yogurt and nutmeg in food processor or blender; process until smooth. Stir in chocolate chips with spoon.

2. Spoon mixture into four plastic pop molds. Place tops on molds; set in provided stand. Freeze 2 hours or until firm. To unmold, briefly run warm water over pop molds until pops loosen. *Makes 4 servings*

Peanut Butter & Jelly Pops: Stir ¼ cup reduced-fat peanut butter in small bowl until smooth; stir in 1 cup nonfat vanilla yogurt. Drop 2 tablespoons strawberry fruit spread on top of mixture; pull spoon back and forth through mixture several times to swirl slightly. Spoon into four pop molds and freeze as directed above.

Blueberry-Lime Pops: Fold ⅓ cup frozen blueberries into 1 cup nonfat Key lime yogurt in small bowl. Spoon into four molds and freeze as directed above.

nutrients per serving:

Calories 103
Calories from Fat 14%
Protein 3g
Carbohydrate 20g
Fiber <1g
Total Fat 2g
Saturated Fat <1g
Cholesterol 1mg
Sodium 37mg

Zucchini

Often mistaken as a cucumber, zucchini is actually a member of the summer squash family. Zucchini has a mild flavor and can be added to almost any dish.

benefits

Besides being low in calories, this versatile vegetable offers plenty of nutrients, including folate, an essential B vitamin, and vitamins A and C, which help to protect the heart and body from cell damage that can lead to heart disease and cancer. Its fiber helps contribute to lower blood cholesterol levels, while its potassium helps maintain a steady heartbeat and keeps blood pressure from rising.

selection and storage

Zucchini is available year-round in most supermarkets. Look for smaller squash for the best flavor. The skin should be unblemished with a deep green or yellow color. It should be firm and feel heavy for its size. Store zucchini in the refrigerator and use within a few days.

preparation and serving tips

The mild flavor of zucchini complements other ingredients in a variety of dishes. It is especially delicious sautéed with tomatoes and onions. Zucchini make a tasty and nutritious addition to lasagnas, marinara sauces and stir-fries. Grate zucchini and add it to quick breads, muffins and cakes to add a ton of moistness without any detectable flavor or added fat.

nutrients per serving:

Zucchini
½ cup cooked slices

Calories 14 *Protein* 1g *Total Fat* 0g
Saturated Fat 0g *Cholesterol* 0mg
Carbohydrate 2g *Dietary Fiber* 1g
Sodium 0mg *Potassium* 240mg
Calcium 16mg *Iron* 0.3mg
Vitamin A 1,005 IU *Vitamin C* 12mg
Folate 25mcg

zucchini cakes

2 cups grated zucchini (2 medium zucchini)
¼ cup all-purpose flour
¼ cup chopped green onions
¼ cup chopped fresh parsley
1 egg
¼ teaspoon garlic salt
  Nonstick cooking spray
  Lemon slices (optional)

1. Combine zucchini, flour, green onions, parsley, egg and garlic salt in food processor or blender; process until well blended.

2. Spray small skillet with nonstick cooking spray; heat over medium heat 1 minute. Spoon 2 tablespoons batter into skillet for each cake; cook 1 to 2 minutes on each side. Serve with lemon slices, if desired.

Makes 8 servings (2 cakes per serving)

nutrients per serving:

Calories 29
Calories from Fat 22%
Protein 2g
Carbohydrate 4g
Fiber <1g
Total Fat <1g
Saturated Fat <1g
Cholesterol 27mg
Sodium 40mg

Glossary

Amino acids: the building blocks of protein. Twenty amino acids are necessary to help the body grow, repair itself and fight disease. Nine of these are considered "essential" because they must come from food you eat, while the body can produce the others.

Anthocyanins: a type of flavonoid responsible for the red and blue pigments found in certain fruits and vegetables. Anthocyanins can help prevent the growth of cancer, lower LDL "bad" cholesterol and prevent clots from forming.

Antioxidant: certain vitamins, minerals and enzymes that help protect cells from damage caused by oxidation, which can result from exposure to tobacco smoke, sunlight, radiation and pollution, as well as aging and illness. Antioxidants offer protection against heart disease, cancer, diabetes, eye disease and numerous other health conditions.

Beta-carotene: a potent antioxidant found in red, orange and yellow plant foods and in some dark green vegetables. It is converted to vitamin A in the body.

Carbohydrate: one of the three major nutrients in food, providing 4 calories per gram. Complex carbohydrates are the primary supplier of energy in the diet and can be found mainly in breads, cereals, pasta, potatoes, squash, beans and peas. Sugars are also known as simple carbohydrates and provide calories (and energy) with few nutrients.

Carotenoids: pigments that give foods their red, orange, and yellow colors. Over 600 different carotenoids have been identified, some of which are powerful antioxidants, including beta-carotene, lutein and lycopene.

Cholesterol: a waxy substance produced by your liver that is part of every cell in the body. The body uses it to manufacture hormones and other essential substances. It is also supplied by the diet when you eat foods from animal sources. Some cholesterol is essential for life, but it can be dangerous as it builds up on artery walls, narrowing blood vessels. LDL (low density lipoprotein), or "bad," cholesterol deposits cholesterol in blood vessels, where it forms plaque that can lead to heart disease. HDL (high density lipoprotein), or "good," cholesterol helps remove cholesterol from the blood and delivers it to the liver, where it can be eliminated.

Cruciferous vegetables: a family of vegetables, including bok choy, broccoli, brussels sprouts, cabbage, cauliflower, kale, mustard greens and turnips, that have cancer-fighting properties. The family is named for its cross-shaped flowers.

Fat: one of the three major nutrients in food, providing 9 calories per gram. Saturated fats, found in butter, stick margarine, meat, poultry skin and whole-fat dairy foods, are solid at room temperature and can raise blood cholesterol levels. Unsaturated fats, found in vegetable oils, nuts, olives and avocados, are liquid at room temperature and help lower blood cholesterol levels.

Fiber: the parts of plants that cannot be digested. Insoluble fiber absorbs water and adds bulk to stools, easing elimination, promoting digestive regularity and providing a feeling of fullness after eating. Soluble fiber forms a gel in the digestive tract and slows the rate of digestion, which helps regulate blood sugar levels and prevent the absorption of cholesterol.

Flavonoids: health-protective substances found in the colorful skins of fruits and vegetables as well as in beverages such as tea, red wine and fruit juices. Their health benefits are similar to those of antioxidants.

Glucose: the basic form of sugars and carbohydrates found in food. It is transported in the blood and used as the primary source of energy. Glucose in the blood is referred to as blood sugar.

Immune function: the body's ability to defend itself against disease and illness.

Legumes: edible seeds that grow in pods; includes beans, peas, lentils and peanuts.

Lutein: a pigment found in foods that are bright yellow, orange and green. Along with zeaxanthin, this carotenoid pigment is linked to a reduced risk of macular degeneration and cataracts.

Lycopene: a powerful antioxidant that gives numerous foods their red color and is especially abundant in tomatoes. It helps protect against prostate cancer, lung cancer and heart disease.

Macular degeneration: deterioration of the central portion of the retina that causes severe vision loss and even blindness, most often in people over 60. Certain nutrients, including vitamins C and E, beta-carotene, zinc and copper, can decrease the risk of vision loss.

Omega-3 fats: a type of unsaturated fat essential for human health that is found in fish, including salmon, tuna and halibut. They are also found other seafood, including algae and krill as well as in some plants and nut oils. These healthy fats play a critical role in brain function, as well as normal growth and development. They help to reduce inflammation that can lead to heart disease, cancer and arthritis.

Pectin: a soluble fiber that helps to lower artery-damaging LDL cholesterol. It is found in most plants but is most abundant in apples, cranberries, plums, grapefruits, lemons and oranges.

Plaque: the fatty substance that builds up in blood vessels. It can constrict blood flow and lead to heart attack and stroke.

Protein: one of the three major nutrients found in food, providing 4 calories per gram. It helps with cell growth and repair as well as fight disease. Vegetable sources include beans, nuts and whole grains. Animal sources include fish, poultry and meat.

Phytochemicals: another name for phytonutrients

Phytonutrients: natural substances found in plants that help protect the plant from disease. In humans, phytonutrients have numerous health-promoting properties; they function as antioxidants to help rid the body of toxins and prevent inflammation.

Polyphenols: natural chemicals in plants, including fruits, vegetables, seeds, legumes and grains, that are responsible for much of their color, flavor and scent. They act as antioxidants and block enzymes that can promote cancer growth.

Triglycerides: the name for fat that travels in your blood, where it is transported to cells and used for energy. High levels of triglycerides can raise your risk of heart disease and may be a sign of metabolic syndrome.

U.S. Dietary Guidelines: official food and nutrition advice for Americans ages 2 and older, jointly published by the U.S. Department of Health and Human Services and the Food and Drug Administration. The guidelines are revised every 5 years, based on the latest scientific research on the effect of food and nutrients on health.

Zeaxanthin: a pigment found in foods that are bright yellow, orange and green. Along with lutein, this pigment in the carotenoid family is linked to a reduced risk of macular degeneration and cataracts.

Metric Conversion Chart

VOLUME MEASUREMENTS (dry)

1/8 teaspoon = 0.5 mL
1/4 teaspoon = 1 mL
1/2 teaspoon = 2 mL
3/4 teaspoon = 4 mL
1 teaspoon = 5 mL
1 tablespoon = 15 mL
2 tablespoons = 30 mL
1/4 cup = 60 mL
1/3 cup = 75 mL
1/2 cup = 125 mL
2/3 cup = 150 mL
3/4 cup = 175 mL
1 cup = 250 mL
2 cups = 1 pint = 500 mL
3 cups = 750 mL
4 cups = 1 quart = 1 L

VOLUME MEASUREMENTS (fluid)

1 fluid ounce (2 tablespoons) = 30 mL
4 fluid ounces (1/2 cup) = 125 mL
8 fluid ounces (1 cup) = 250 mL
12 fluid ounces (1 1/2 cups) = 375 mL
16 fluid ounces (2 cups) = 500 mL

WEIGHTS (mass)

1/2 ounce = 15 g
1 ounce = 30 g
3 ounces = 90 g
4 ounces = 120 g
8 ounces = 225 g
10 ounces = 285 g
12 ounces = 360 g
16 ounces = 1 pound = 450 g

DIMENSIONS

1/16 inch = 2 mm
1/8 inch = 3 mm
1/4 inch = 6 mm
1/2 inch = 1.5 cm
3/4 inch = 2 cm
1 inch = 2.5 cm

OVEN TEMPERATURES

250°F = 120°C
275°F = 140°C
300°F = 150°C
325°F = 160°C
350°F = 180°C
375°F = 190°C
400°F = 200°C
425°F = 220°C
450°F = 230°C

BAKING PAN SIZES

Utensil	Size in Inches/Quarts	Metric Volume	Size in Centimeters
Baking or Cake Pan (square or rectangular)	8×8×2	2 L	20×20×5
	9×9×2	2.5 L	23×23×5
	12×8×2	3 L	30×20×5
	13×9×2	3.5 L	33×23×5
Loaf Pan	8×4×3	1.5 L	20×10×7
	9×5×3	2 L	23×13×7
Round Layer Cake Pan	8×1½	1.2 L	20×4
	9×1½	1.5 L	23×4
Pie Plate	8×1¼	750 mL	20×3
	9×1¼	1 L	23×3
Baking Dish or Casserole	1 quart	1 L	—
	1½ quart	1.5 L	—
	2 quart	2 L	—